# THE ACHIEVING GHETTO

by

Eugene P. Foley

The National Press Inc., Washington, D.C.

Copyright © 1968 by Eugene P. Foley
All Rights Reserved

Library of Congress
     Catalog Card Number 67-30360

Published by:
     The National Press Inc.
     128 C Street N. E.
     Washington, D. C. 20002

# CONTENTS

# INTRODUCTION

I cannot recall precisely the point in time I resolved to write this book. To the best of my memory, it occurred in September 1966, following a meeting at the White House of about twelve top Administration officials convened to draft a new program for the cities; more particularly, for the ghettos. Neither the President nor the Vice President were in attendance. The Bureau of the Budget (BOB) had prepared a list of approximately fifteen "new" proposals as a framework for such a new program. It contained the usual recommendations for studies, reviews, analyses, and appointment of task forces, which are the standard strategies of the Bureau for meeting public or Congressional pressure on hot issues. I observed in my usually unpleasant direct way that none of the proposals were new or original and that they contained not the terms of a new program but rather of surrender and that the heart of the cities' problems lay in the unemployment of the hard core unemployed. More specifically, this meant Negroes, Puerto Ricans, and Mexican-Americans. I knew this

3

would bring me in direct conflict with Charles Schultze, the Director of the Budget Bureau; but I felt I had delayed doing so long enough.

Schultze, a warm, friendly, highly talented person, without conscious prejudice, a man with a great sense of humor and a strong feeling for social justice, had once told me: "Jobs won't do anything for Negroes. What did jobs do for them during World War II? Negroes had jobs then, but what problems did they solve? After the war they were back to their old ways. There is not much that can be done with this generation of Negroes other than education."

Of the twelve top officials there, only then Attorney General Nicholas Katzenbach and Secretary of Labor Willard Wirtz expressed their agreement with me. In fact, Wirtz recommended and Katzenbach and I supported the notion that the Budget Bureau's proposals be redirected to face squarely the hard core unemployment problem. There was some vague general agreement with this idea, the details of which could be discussed at another meeting. I was not invited to subsequent meetings, which never really bothered me because I never expected anything to develop out of them. Nothing ever did.

The point of relating this incident is that sometime in September 1966, it finally sunk into me that if I were ever going to have my deeply felt point of view on "jobs in the ghettos" fully considered, I would have to appeal to an audience wider than Government policy-makers. That meant a book.

I come down a little hard on the BOB in this book, and I think it is therefore incumbent upon me to attempt some balancing of the score as far as the Bureau is concerned. The Budget Bureau is made up of the brightest, hardest working talent in Washington. The Directors of the Bureau in the Kennedy and Johnson Administrations have not only been outstanding scholars but also outstanding Budget Directors. They and the people who work for them are the favorite "whipping boys" for every government Department and Agency, every special interest group, and just about every Congressman and Senator. The reason for this is rather simple; it is among the Bureau's responsibilities, as coordinator for all legislative proposals, to say "No" for the President day after day and to serve as the President's "lightning rod."

Thus, a book suggesting criticism of the BOB will excite little attention in the Executive Office Building. Nevertheless, I resolved to write my ideas on jobs for Negroes into a book not only because I feel strongly that Schultze and the Bureau are wrong and that the issue is urgent but also because this issue helps illustrate another idea long held by me;viz., the Budget Bureau is the wrong mechanism to use in assigning national priorities.

Let me make it clear that I fully agree that some agency or group must be responsible for setting priorities and that this agency or group must be responsible to the President alone. The reason for this is that the built-in bias of each government Department and Agency and of each of the Bureaus within each Department and Agency is so strong that the annual recommendations for new appropriations and new legislation are far beyond the capacity of this country to absorb. Some agency must set the priorities and allocate the resources accordingly.

While it is rather obvious that the various Departments and Agencies are compartmentalized into parochial interests and pressure groups, it is not so immediately apparent that the Bureau of the Budget and its colleagues in government opinion-making and priority-setting are also. I have in mind the Treasury Department, Council of Economic Advisers, and Federal Reserve Board. These agencies are limited by the rigid methodology of a single academic. discipline; viz., that of economics.

Economists (with a few exceptions, such as John K. Galbraith and James Tobin) have a built-in bias to see social problems in wholly rational, nonemotional, and static terms because they are preoccupied and almost solely focussed on the concepts of macro-economics; that is, they are pre-eminently concerned with the Gross National Product, the economics of the country as a whole rather than any of its industrial, geographical, or social subdivisions. It was economists in the first blush of success of the New Economics that led President Kennedy to state in his famous Yale speech that the national economy and budget were matters of technique that could be made almost self-operable if only old prejudices would give way. Unquestionably, the New Economics has proved to be a dramatically historical success with respect to reviving a sluggish national economy; but what about values; what about the justice of distributing national resources solely in terms of the status quo; what, in short, about priorities? The economists in their macro-economic cloisters presume these will be taken care of in the long run.

I have always been impressed with the encyclopedic knowledge of human nature Harry Hopkins evidenced in the midst of the white man's depression with the curt observation, "People eat in the short run," and that of the father of the New Economics, Lord Keynes,

"In the long run people die." Unfortunately, people are currently dying in short run riots and many black people are not eating very well in the long run. The Budget Bureau's economic tools do not measure these things. The tools of the other social sciences are needed in order to gauge more accurately the real costs and benefits of social and economic progress. Nothing better illustrates the Budget Bureau's naive handling of complex social problems than the blind faith it reposed in the "wonder tools" of Program Planning and Budgeting Systems. This is really the subject for another paper but suffice it to say that Program Budgeting of the McNamara kind, with all due respect to the brilliant creativeness of the former Secretary of Defense, most easily applies to defense strategies and tactics because its costs and benefits are nearly all quantifiable and therefore measureable. This is not true of the social agencies. As a matter of fact, while I recommend the creation of a new Presidential Policy Group made up of representatives from all the social sciences as well as different economic interests, it is my contention that the best program budgeters in domestic programs are good, hardheaded, pragmatic, progressive politicians.

There is something of an earlier progenitor to this book than the incident I have just mentioned. In the spring of 1964, I was serving as Administrator of the Small Business Administration and had begun a series of experimental programs involving Negro businessmen. Since this was a part of the Negro Community which had not yet been dissected, bisected, studied to death, and analyzed, I began to be looked upon as something of an expert on the subject. Eventually, I was asked to contribute a paper on the Negro businessman for a special issue on the American Negro, published by Daedalus, the quarterly publication of the American Academy of Arts and Sciences. One of the more surprising and refreshing stipulations for each paper was that it include specific, concrete proposals to help correct the problems which the author had observed. Since I had established that almost all Negro-owned businesses were inside the ghetto rather than outside, one obvious new problem, or solution as the case may be, was the economic development of the ghetto. My research assistants and I canvassed the literature on anything conceivably bearing on this subject and about the only things we could find were nonpublished circulars and tracts of the Black Muslims and other Black Nationalist groups. Time prevented me from developing any economic proposals in depth for that paper, but the subject continued to interest me.

9

Subsequently, I was appointed Assistant Secretary of Commerce for Economic Development, with responsibility for the economic rehabilitation of the nation's "depressed areas." For various reasons which are not necessary to detail here, the "depressed areas" programs have predominantly been directed to the *white* depressed areas of our country—Appalachia, the rural South, the upper Great Lakes areas, and others. By this time I had spent too much time in Harlem, Watts, Bedford Stuyvesant, Birmingham, Oakland, Atlanta, Chicago, North and South Philadelphia, Jackson, Mississippi, Hunter's Point, Northside Detroit, and other Negro ghettos not to ask the elemental question, "Why should these programs not be designed to rehabilitate Negro depressed areas?" Receiving no answers and absolutely no encouragement, it began to dawn on me that I would have to supply the answer, in part, if not in whole. That meant a book.

This book is about the economic development of the Negro ghettos in our urban areas. Puerto Ricans, Mexican-Americans, Indian and Chinese also live in ghettos. I have not written about these even though they should be written about. I have chosen to write about the Negro ghettos in urban areas because it involves more people than the others and because I have been more personally involved in those problems than in the others. While this book is hardly the last word on the economic development of the Negro ghetto, it is, as I have indicated, just about the first word. If it stimulates further thought and hopefully some action, I have at least accomplished something.

Who to thank for assistance and ideas must be difficult for every writer. Recognizing that I shall unjustly leave some deserving soul's name out of print, I must first of all include Lynn Dixon, Ruth Gould, Fay Brisk, and the tireless Carol Moody, all of whom helped me beyond measure with my paper on the Negro businessman; Randolph Tyus of the Small Business Administration, who took it upon himself to introduce me to real live Negro businessmen all over the country; Ed Rosa, Marty Wolf, Doris Hall, and Stan Gallagher of the Philadelphia office of the SBA, who stuck their respective necks out with respect to certain career government officials to help me gather information and conduct experiments with Negro businessmen; Berkely Berrell, President of the National Business League, an association of Negro businessmen, for arranging meetings with that organization around the country as well as for an award from it; Austin Norris, an authentic Philadelphia lawyer wiser than most Philadelphia lawyers; and Dr. Haym Jaffe and the Drexel Institute of Philadelphia for their close cooperation.

Also, a first rate establishment economist (and a first rate guy) John Kain of Harvard, who has always delighted in attacking the theories that underlie this book, and thus sharpened them, and several more first rate establishment economists who served with me in the Commerce Department and supported me in my various experiments in the ghetto, despite the lack of the profession's approbation, Ben Chinitz, Martin McGuire, Anthony Pascal, and Bob Rauner; my Oakland crew, Doug Castle, Andrew Bennett, Blair Butterworth, Dick Daschback, Ann Gould, Tom Shea, and George Karras, whose collective overtime spent in our Oakland experiment would stun, shock, and properly embarrass the American taxpaper; my typists, whose skill and devotion could be exceeded only by their beauty, Marina Gentilini and Maureen McNellis; and my Administrative Assistants in the SBA and Commerce Department, Frances Pappas, Frances Gray, and Eva Middleton, who served far above and way beyond the call of Civil Service duty and whose patience would tire Job.

Above all, there are two people to whom I must pay special thinks. First, Mrs. Diana Zentay, who helped me prepare the materials for this book. If I were to say all the things about this marvelous person, I would conceivably open myself to an Alienation of Affections suit on the part of her husband.

Second, Amory Bradford. Consider the probability of a former general manager of the New York Times teaming up with an Irish-Catholic lawyer from the Minnesota farm country to conduct a pioneering experiment on hiring the long-term Negro unemployed in Oakland, California, spending the better part of a year in uniting the extreme opposite ends of Oakland's economic and social structure into a combined social effort, making it a signal success, and you can only explain it by the peculair daring, determination, and dedication to one's beliefs that is the hallmark of a long line of New England Congregational ministers by the name of Bradford.

And finally, my publisher, Jim Clay, who encouraged me and urged me to put my studies into book form.

(s) Eugene P. Foley

# CHAPTER I

# THE ACHIEVING
# GHETTO

"Does there attach to my ancient race some venerable curse by which we are to be...without the right to
choose our course in public affairs?" 1/

\*   \*   \*   \*   \*   \*

"They're raiding Noblett's.'" "Suddenly, with a
tremendous crash, the plate glass front of Noblett's,
a confectioner's,...smashed onto the pavement. A cas-
cade of sweets spilled out and men, women and children scooped up handfuls of chocolates, Turkish de-
light, glacier mints, fruit bonbons. Boxes were ripped
open and strewn over the pavement. The mob went
wild with excitement. As the news of the spoils available spread rapidly, the crowds swelled in size...In
the middle of the looting somebody shouted, "the
soldiers are coming.'"2/

The ancient race referred to was not Negro
and the looting scene was not Watts. But Watts
and Harlem and Hunters Point are directly
linked to the looting scene which took place
on Sackville Street (now O'Connell Street)

15

downtown Dublin, during the Easter Rebellion
'of 1916. And the ancient race, upon whom the
"venerable curse" lay, as it has upon every
ethnic group at one time or another and thus
links the human family, was the Irish.

The Irish-American, like most white Americans, is troubled by America's racial problems.
He knows that what the Negroes demand is in-
herent in American democracy but he is also
familiar with his own immigrant background
and says to himself, "my ancestors had it as bad
as the Negroes and still made it, why can't
they?" As an Irish American housewife of
thirty in Boston said:

> "I don't understand them (Negroes) at all...They
> want to go here and there, and send their children
> everywhere...You'd think Negroes were the only peo-
> ple in America that have a tough time. What about the
> rest of us?...
>
> My father couldn't find a job either...I remember my
> mother telling us how he walked and walked, practi-
> cally begging for work...The day he applied for relief
> was the saddest day of his life. It broke him. He hated
> himself ever after...He was plain scared for the rest
> of his life. ...
>
> That's the trouble, though, with Negores..they only
> know how to ask, not go out and earn. I know they had
> it bad here, but so did we all..."3/

The woman is right—the Irish did have it
bad, as did the Jews, Greeks, Poles, and Italians, and all other ethnic groups. But these

16

others had a system of social organization that the Negroes have never had in their strong family traditions and their churches and synagogues. [In addition, each of the other ethnic groups were inspired and motivated by an honored culture which stimulated high aspiration and expectations as well as a lofty sense of self-esteem.] One thing more those groups possessed which Negroes have lacked until very recently and has badly needed in order to protect themselves in a hostile environment — group solidarity.

Moynihan and Glazer have said that the most remarkable thing about America's famous "melting pot" is that it never really happened.[4] That is, the various ethnic groups never "melted" together; they remained remarkably separate — and for good reasons. Ethnic groups have always banded together because of the strength an individual gains from associating with a community with which he can totally identify. Individuals in this country developed in groups and the group mediated between the individual and the larger society. Above all, group solidarity reduced the powerlessness of the group and, thereby, that of the individual. It is precisely this which is taking place in the civil rights movement today.

For the great part of its history, civil rights was a white liberal's cause. Liberals expounded

17

the moral *basis* for human *rights* in economic institution and activities. But recently Negro involvement in civil rights has taken a new turn. David Danzig of Columbia University has been one of the first to note this development.

> "The goal of the liberals in the Civil Rights movement has been primarily to change the formal social order—not the personal human relations or those of their children—they support civil rights as a necessary part of a moral democratic order. *The Negro movement, on the other hand, is a self-interest movement which is for civil rights because it serves Negro welfare.*"5/

The code name of this new Negro movement is "Black Power."

"Black Power" in 1967, became a major issue on the national civil rights scene. It has been defined, redefined, argued, and reargued. The reason Stokely Carmichael's phrase caught on so quickly is because it captured in two words the current Negro mood of angry impatience and growing racial pride, a mood that said, "to really share in American life, we Negroes must have power."

The power the overwhelming body of Negroes seek is not the power of violence or of hate, but the power of constructive pride and group achievement. Black Power means to the vast majority of Negroes what James Farmer says it should mean: "It should preach self respect and group pride to those who have been without respect and pride."

It is said in international affairs that "a Nation seeks not friends, but mutual interests." The Negroes have arrived at just that degree of political and social sophistication. It is crucial to peaceful race relations that we understand this and understand what directly follows from this; viz, the ghetto is here to stay for a long, long time.

The idea that the ghetto is here to stay for a long, long time is hardly a pleasant thought nor very popular. But I am not alone in this view. St. Clair Drake co-auther of the *Black Metropolis*, and one of the keen, knowledgeable observers, not only of ghetto life, but of American life, voiced these same thoughts, in the Fall of 1965.[6]

"Few Negroes believe that Black Ghettos will disappear within the next two decades despite much talk about "open occupancy" and "freedom of residence." There is an increasing tendency among Negroes to discuss what the quality of life could be within Negro Communities as they grow larger and larger...

It is probable that the Black Belts of America will increase in size rather than decrease during the next decade, for no city seems likely to commit itself to "open occupancy" ...*And even if a race-free market were to appear Negroes would remain segregated unless drastic changes took place in the job ceiling and income gap.* Controlled integration will probably continue, with a few upper- and upper-middle class Negroes trickling into the suburbs and into carefully regulated mixed neighborhoods and mixed buildings within the city limits. *The basic problem of the next decade will be how to change Black Ghettos into relatively stable and attractive "colored Communities."*

Ralph Ellison, author if *The Invisible Man,* told a Senate Subcommittee in September, 1966, much the same:

"It is a misunderstanding to assume that Negroes want to break out of Harlem. They want to transform Harlem, the Harlems of their country. These places are precious to them...People want Harlem improved not torn down. They want Harlem to remain as a base, just as people in other sections want their old blocks to remain as home base.7

I have talked to many Negroes on this subject since I first started having my disquieting thoughts and I have not found one Negro who really disagrees with me. The people who really disagree are the middle class and upper class white liberals in Government and academic life who display what I think is a form of cultural arrogance towards Negroes, who seem to insist that the ghetto must develop in their own image and likeness. It still does not seem to have dawned on the white liberal why Negroes resent him so, why they resent this patronizing attitude as to the Negro communities' values and goals. The "ghettoization" of the Negro has resulted in the emergence of a ghetto subculture with a distinctive ethos, most pronounced

20

perhaps in Harlem, but recognizable in all
Negro neighborhoods.

> "(Harlems) are where they (Negroes) have dreamed,
> where they have lived, where they have loved, where
> they have worked out their life as they could...Harlem
> is a place where our folklore is preserved and trans-
> formed. It is the place where the body of Negro myth
> and legend thrives. It is a place where our styles, musi-
> cal styles, the many styles of Negro life, find continuity
> and metamorphoris."8

This is the world in which the upper classes
wince as at an embarrassment, and which race
leaders point to as proof that Negroes have
been victimized. But for the masses of the
ghetto dwellers this is a warm and familiar
milieu, preferable to the sanitary coldness of
middle-class neighborhoods.

This is a highly delicate subject because
stating that the ghetto is here to stay for a long
time appears defeatist, seems to suggest a
separate but equal doctrine. Let me make it
very clear. I do not oppose open occupancy; I
favor it. I am not against Negroes moving to
the suburbs; I am for it. I am not for any
lessening of pressure or zeal on fulfilling the
dream of American democracy. I am, however,
very much for understanding what may be
termed the social-group or subcultural aspects
of our racial problems and attempting thereby
to find new opportunities for their solution.

21

It is the middle class that assimilates in our country. It is the middle class that embarks upon the so-called mainstream of American life. Very briefly stated, then, I believe, strange as it may seem, that the ghetto itself can offer opportunities to develop a Negro middle class that not only will accelerate Negro welfare but integration as well.

"Black Power", Dave Danzig has pointed out, "begins with a belief in the importance of Negro solidarity. It takes the reality of the ghetto as its starting point and would use the ghettos' strength to improve the conditions of life for the mass of Negroes."[9] This is exactly what every other ethnic group has done. Consider the Irish.

The American Irish began arriving in large numbers in the 1840's. They—as most immigrant groups before and after—occupied the lowest rung of the social and economic ladder, only to be pushed up later by the arrival of new groups and pulled up by their own progress. Each Irishman had, along with treasured items from home, a deep hope that life for him would be better here, or, if not for him for his children. Negroes, bear in mind, were never offered that hope.

Beginning in 1820, 19 million immigrants came to the U.S. in less than 100 years; 1.7 million of these were from Ireland who arrived between 1840 and 1860. Unable to afford adequate housing, the Irish were forced to accept crowded lining in "shanties." The home and the church were the centers of life in the community. The style of living was a warm, gregarious one which developed strong family and neighborhood loyalties. The family unit was a cohesive force in the Irish-American development. Men were judged not only on their own merits, but on the merits of the entire family. Family pride, a strong sense of obligation to maintain the honor of one's family, was a cherished value. The Church was the great common denominator and rallying point. Aside from purely religious aspects, it was the center of much of the social activity of the Irish colony.

The educational problems of the Irish were much the same as Negroes. Textbooks were written in terms that were not understandable to the children. Irish children were unfamiliar with Anglo-Saxon names and references much as Negroes are puzzled by the white middle class quality that permeates today's textbooks.

Those outside the Irish community viewed it in much the same way as outsiders today view the Negro community — a group of trouble-makers, posing problems in housing, police, and schools which meant higher tax rates and heavier burdens in support of the poorhouse.

Moreover, the "Irish did not seem to practice thrift, self-denial, and other virtues desirable in the 'worthy, laboring poor.' "[10]

Native citizens greeted the massive influx of Irish with resentment, anxiety and anger. Public order, public health, and public education were thrown into disarray. The immigrant Irish were a threat to the civilized amenities, disrupting neighborhoods, and interrupting the pursuit of happiness. In 1872, a book was published called "The Dangerous Classes of New York"[11] referred primarily to the Irish. Theodore Roosevelt said in 1882 that the average Irishman was "a low, venal, corrupt and unintellignet brute."[12] Irving Kristol contends that alcoholism wreaked far greater havoc among the Immigrant Irish than all the drugs and stimulants do today among Negroes. He says most of the Irish slums were dirtier and more crowded (if we are to believe contemporary reports) than today's Negro slums.[13] But with it all, the Irish had group solidarity and they had numbers.

In 1850, 26 percent of New York City's population had been born in Ireland. If their children and other second—and third—generation Irish are included, New York was more than one-third Irish. Boston also showed a phenomenal rise of Irish immigrants. In 1854, the Irish-born population of that city was only one in fifty. Ten years later, the ratio was one in five. The political power which the Irish attained in these two cities is particularly understandable in light of these figures. The Irish had an advantage over other immigrant groups in sheer numbers. In Boston, they were for 40 years the only alien immigrant group there. By the time the Italians, Russian Jews, Lithuanians, and other groups began to arrive in the 1880's, the Irish were already almost a majority of the entire city. Group solidarity and large numbers had offered the Irish their unique opportunity to confront the hostile Anglo-Saxon environment.

The political rise of the Irish and the consequent economic rise began with their taking over the Democratic Party. Through a network of clubhouses, family loyalties and a hierarchy of party committees, the Irish converted the party into a shadow government. The political machine, as it came to be called, waited patiently in the wings for the real thing.

"The immigrant (Irish) laborer desperate tor a job to feed his family, the immigrant family quarreling with the landlord, the widowed mother deprived of her income, the injured workman, the sweatshop employee, and the truant boy in trouble with the police needed someone or some agency more compassionate and helpful than the routine 'good government'

25

> ...Moreover, if the different levels did exercise positive power, it was usually on behalf of businessmen by granting land subsidies to railroad companies or using police to break strikes."[14/]

The Irish presence was particularly felt in New York City politics. In 1855, for instance, New York City had 1,000 policemen — 26 percent of the force — who were natives of Ireland. Forty-five percent of the Chicago police force that year had Irish last names. In Boston, the first Irishman was on the police force in 1851 but it wasn't until 1886 that an Irishman was elected mayor. By 1899, the Irish had the majority of seats on the City Council.

In New York City, the Irish were deeply involved with Tammany Hall, the queen of political machines. From 1865, when it helped elect that city's first Irish mayor, until 1950, that organization had much to do with who was on the Board of Aldermen, who was mayor, and who was governor.

Tammany was effective not only in getting people elected. It was the indispensable means by which the Irish immigrants were provided that most precious of all commodities — a job. The Irish attacked vehemently any proposal that threatened to reduce or eliminate job opportunities for their kin — as for instance, the Civil Service Reform Law.

26

"This civil service law is the biggest fraud of the age ... There can't be no real patriotism while it lasts. How are you going to interest our young men in their country if you have no offices to give them when they work for their party?[15]

"There's just one issue that would set this country on fire. The Democratic Party should say in the first plank of its platform: 'We hereby declare, in national convention assembled, that the paramount issue now, always and forever, is the abolition of the iniquitous and villainous civil service laws which are destroyin' all patriotism, ruinin' the country and takin' away good jobs from them that earn them.'"[16]

Jobs — that was the immigrants priority concern. The machine's importance lay in providing political means to economic ends. They were able to begin large public construction projects that involved many men with only rudimentary skills, jobs that men from agricultural backgrounds — most of the immigrants were — could do. And there were no unions to exclude them.

The family friendships and neighborhood loyalties that made the Irish so suited to poltics were viewed not as a struggle to obtain the best possible government *but as a struggle among competing groups.* Once in office, the winning group had every right to reward its own. What other people called graft was, to the Irish, simply a compromise between the

27

formal rules of the political system and the facts of life as they knew them.

Those Irish who had gained prominence affected all Irish, for the entire group—even those who had not yet "arrived"—felt proud. They felt part of that success. And those who had not yet "made it" were instilled with even more hope and assurance that they, too, could accomplish their dreams. (Well do I remember much later, cold, snowy winter nights in the 1930's in a small Minnesota farm town and how my mother encouraged my father and lifted all of us with the latest success stories of the Kennedys of Boston. How Senator Edward Brooke must fire the flames in some young Negro's heart in Southern Alabama today.)

With the coming of other ethnic groups in large numbers, thus diluting their political effectiveness, the American Irish reached a political plateau in 1900 that they were not to advance much beyond until the Depression brought their party into power. But,

> "By the turn of the century, the Irish were no longer represented on the stage as dressed in rags and living in shanties or slums . . . the Irish, in short, stood at the opening of the twentieth century with a foot in each world. The desire to join the "ins" conflicted with the desire to lead the 'outs'. The wish to climb socially ran counter to the impulse to champion the rebellious, restless poor. The options for individual Irishmen

28

were numerous: conventional success or frustrated insurgency, individual assimilation or the chauvinism of the Irish Community, bleached — out respectability or labor radicalism, adherence to the political machine or acceptance of good government ('goo goo') values, the American-style idealism of Gibbons and Ireland or the clerical reaction in Corrigan and McQuaid. They had come a long way in seventy years."[17]

They still had a long way to go but the majority were moving into the great middle range of society and the economy. They had one foot in the lower middle class, but their hands reached up many rungs of the ladder and included already a few Irish millionaires. Most of all, William Shannon says, "they were important in shoring up the values of the business community because they were the small Capitalists and the expectant capitalists."[18]

The Great Depression brought the Irish into national political offices but it also shocked and disoriented millions of middle-class and working-class Irish. It took most of another generation but gradually the Irish-American dropped the hyphen, invaded the Republican Party and the Country Club, attended Harvard, forgot his Irish poetry, sang once a year or at an occasional drunk Irish songs composed by Jewish Americans, struggled to remember his father's struggles much less his

29

grandfather's or the 75 years of organized Irish-Catholic activity to protect and promote the Irish-Catholic, but oh, so proud, at how far he had come on his own!

The first Negroes arrived as slaves in 1619. The African society from which they were torn was highly organized. Each facet of life —eating, drinking, working, sex, relaxing, sleeping—was carefully regulated by detailed ritual and rules. Sociologists have estimated that the wrenching of Negroes from these societies and throwing them into a totally rootless situation was more damaging to them than any physical pain they subsequently suffered.

Not only was the Negro not allowed to retain the ways of his tribe, he was denied his family and even his name. He was denied the opportunity to learn; in many states educating slaves was against the law. He was placed in a completely dependent position. Thus a bearable life for the Negro depended not on initiative and drive, not on nurturing and seeking to fulfill a goal, but on obeying, on being subservient. This was the beginning of a racism that has marred this country's history. It has been part of the American consciousness and value system ever since.

Colonists were eager to maintain the slavery system primarily for economic reasons. That

30

the Negro was essential to the colonial economy was his curse. Most men could not afford white indentured servants; blacks were cheap and could not leave. (It is important to note that part of this system, a part which one must remember when considering why Negroes have not attained economic and political power, involved assuming—and reinforcing the assumption—that Negroes were inferior. It is a common psychological phenomena that when enough people assume something about a person, he begins to adopt that "role". Overcoming that "role" has not been an easy task.

Unlike other immigrants, the Negro was never able to build a community based on ethnic unity that sustained late arrivals and aided their adjustment. Indeed, each new Negro was stripped of his heritage and his person, as all others arriving before him had been. There was no escape. The Negro's very color served as a most effective prohibition to progress. The plantation system both before and after the Civil War deprived the Negro of a family life.

Jobs, I have pointed out, were the immigrant's priority concern. It was this group concern and the resulting competition between groups that historically kept the northern Negro out of the better job opportunities. The simultaneous influx, in the 19th century, of freed and fugitive slaves, on the one hand, and foreign immigrants, on the other, resulted in prejudice, lawlessness, crime, poverty, and race riots.

The decade of the 1820's, I have elsewhere noted, witnessed the first great confrontation of free Negroes and immigrants, a confrontation which continued with rising intensity and without abatement for the next hundred years, until Congress, in the early 1920's passed the Immigration Exclusion Acts.[19]

In Philadelphia, for instance, the first race riots were held in 1829, recurred frequently until 1840, and really did not cease until some time after the Civil War. And in New York City the famous draft riot of 1863 was to a larger degree provoked by the Irish immigrants' antipathy to Negroes. Archbishop John Hughes warned the War Department in 1861 that his Roman Catholic flock was "willing to fight to the death for the support of the Constitution, the government, and the laws of the country," but not "for the abolition of slavery."[20] The Emancipation Proclamation and the importation of Negroes to break a stevedore's strike caused great Irish resentment. On 13 July 1863, while the names of draftees, largely the low-income Irish because of the provisions providing for exemption upon the payment of $300.00, were being drawn, the provost marshal was driven from his office by a mob.

> "Rioters controlled the streets during the better part of four days and nights, sacking shops and the homes of anti-slavery leaders, gutting saloons, lynching or torturing Negroes who fell into their clutches, burning mansions and a colored orphan asylum."[21/]

It was not until troops were poured into the city that order was restored, after the loss of several hundred people killed and wounded, and a million dollars in property damage. The very perceptive early sociologist, W. E. B. DuBois, spelled the problem out very clearly. Noting the rapid economic changes which accompanied the growing industrialization of the American economy, he said:

> "The new industries attracted the Irish, Germans, and other immigrants; Americans too, were fleeing to the city and soon to natural race antipathies was added a determined effort to displace Negro Labor—an effort which had the aroused prejudice of many of the better classes, and the poor quality of the new black immigrants to give it aid and comfort. To all this was soon added a problem of crime and poverty. Numerous complaints of petty thefts, housebreaking, and assaults on peaceful citizens were traced to certain classes of Negroes. ...a mass of poverty-stricken, ignorant fugitives and ill trained freed men had rushed to the city, swarmed in the vile slums which the rapidly growing city furnished, and met in

33

> social and economic competition equally igno-
> rant but more vigorous foreigners. These for-
> eigners outbid them at work, beat them on the
> streets, and were enabled to do this by the pre-
> judice which Negro crime and the anti-slavery
> sentiment had aroused in the city.[22/]

The foreigners outbid the Negroes not only at work but also at the hiring halls. In the 1890's Samuel Gompers urged affiliates of the American Federation of Labor to end discrimination. In his report to the AFL Convention of 1900, he warned that unless the Negro was allowed to organize, and the white worker showed him friendship, there could be "no question but that they will not only be forced down in the economic scale and used against an effort made by us for our economic and social advancement, but race prejudice will be made more bitter."[23/]

In 1902, the AFL decided to give charters to central labor unions, local unions or Federal labor unions, composed exclusively of Negroes. But in 1935, when a small group of Negro employees of the Pullman Company established the Brotherhood of Sleeping Car Porters, the AFL would not give them a charter, and did not until 1936.

The result of this continual combat was not only to restrict job opportunities for the Negroes to the most menial and unrewarding tasks but also to reinforce the Negroes' sense of inferiority. Furthermore, it divided the Negro who was a native of the City from the Negro newly arrived, because the latter's migration North in larger numbers, beginning in the 1890's, caused the native whites to withdraw privileges from the former.

> "The old colored citizens of Philadelphia resented this, placed the blame at the migrant's door and stood aloof from him. Negro preachers invited the new arrivals into the church, but many of the congregations made him know he was not wanted. In some cases the church split over the matter, the migrants and their sympathizers withdrawing and forming a church for themselves."[24]

Other ethnic groups had similar troubles — German Jews, for instance, resented Eastern European Jews. But in this case, the large numbers of each group, the existence of a strong and ancient culture, and the possession of abilities and crafts needed in the American economy, gave even divided groups a unity and strength which Negroes failed to develop.

In short, the unceasing and unbalanced social and economic competition between each influx of Negroes and each wave of immigrants, together with the relatively insignificant family and social institutions and resulting lack of political strength of the former compared to the latter, as well as the accompanying discountenance and repression from all whites,

35

kept the Negroes from developing as a group and prevented, thereby, any significant achievement or assimilation by Negroes throughout the entire nineteenth century.

While Negroes have been here longer than most immigrant groups, they did not begin arriving in the cities until this century. Table I illustrates that Negroes in 1960 were one-quarter of Philadelphis's population; the Irish were a quarter in 1900. Negroes were 14% of New York City's population in 1960, something the Irish had attained in the middle of the last century.

Table II is another way of illustrating the migration. Between 1940 and 1950, the South

TABLE I
NEGRO POPULATION AND POPULATION OF IRISH ORIGIN, 1890-1960
Percentage

Note: Irish origin refers to persons born in Ireland or born in the U.S. of Irish parentage.

| Year | Boston | | Philadelphia | | Chicago | | New York City | |
|------|--------|-------|--------------|-------|---------|-------|---------------|-------|
|      | Irish  | Negro | Irish | Negro | Irish | Negro | Irish | Negro |
| 1890 | 32.9 | 1.8 | 21.6 | 3.8 | 14.3 | 1.4 | 38.0 | 2.6* |
| 1900 | 40.4 | 2.1 | 24.7 | 4.8 | 15.0 | 1.8 | 25.3 | 1.8 |
| 1910 | 23.0 | 2.0 | 12.8 | 5.5 | 7.6 | 2.0 | 12.2 | 1.9 |
| 1920 | 23.4 | 2.9 | 12.2 | 7.4 | 7.4 | 4.1 | 11.0 | 2.7 |
| 1930 | 20.4 | 2.6 | 9.4 | 11.3 | 5.7 | 6.9 | 8.8 | 4.7 |
| 1940 | 16.3 | 3.1 | 6.6 | 13.0 | 4.4 | 8.2 | 7.0 | 6.1 |
| 1950 | 3.5 | 5.0 | 1.2 | 18.2 | .84 | 13.6 | 1.8 | 9.5 |
| 1960 | 10.7 | 9.1 | 2.9 | 26.4 | 2.4 | 22.9 | 4.0 | 14.0 |

*In 1890, only the Borough of Manhattan was included. The following years include all five boroughs.

Source: U.S. Census Bureau, Office of Population

36

| Region | 1950-60 | | | | 1940-50 | | | |
|---|---|---|---|---|---|---|---|---|
| | White | | Nonwhite | | White | | Nonwhite | |
| | Number | Percent[2] | Number | Percent[2] | Number | Percent[3] | Number | Percent[3] |
| United States- | 2,588 | 1.9 | 28 | 0.2 | 1,522 | 1.3 | -160 | -1.2 |
| Northeast | -206 | -0.6 | 541 | 26.0 | -173 | -0.5 | 483 | 34.3 |
| North Central | -679 | -1.6 | 558 | 23.8 | -948 | -2.5 | 632 | 42.0 |
| South | 52 | .1 | -1,457 | -14.1 | -538 | -1.7 | -1,597 | -16.0 |
| West | 3,421 | 18.4 | 385 | 39.0 | 3,181 | 23.8 | 323 | 60.5 |

[1]Includes net immigration from abroad.
[2]Base is 1950 population.
[3]Base is 1940 population.

SOURCE: *Estimates of the Components of Population Change by Color, for States; 1950 to 1960,
Current Population Reports, Population Estimates,* Series P-25, No. 247, Apr. 2, 1962,
table 4 (U.S. Bureau of the Census). Includes 1940-50 data.

lost 16% of its Negroes, and between 1950 and 1960, it lost 14%.

Table III compares the percentages of Negroes and whites living in urban areas. Twenty-seven percent of all Negroes lived in cities in 1910; the percentage was 73 by 1960. And in 1910 only about 12% of all Negroes lived outside of the South.

Table IV shows the high percentage of Negroes living in northern cities who were born in the South.

Most urban Negroes, therefore, have been in cities less than 20 years; almost all have been in cities less than 50 years. The Negro, in short, is the latest immigrant.

Despite the growing concentration of Negroes in the northern urban areas, this latest

TABLE III

PERCENTAGE OF NEGRO AND WHITE POPULATION LIVING IN
URBAN AREAS, BY REGION, CONTERMINOUS
UNITED STATES, 1910-60

| YEAR | United States | | South | | North and West | |
|---|---|---|---|---|---|---|
| | Negro | White | Negro | White | Negro | White |
| 1910 .................... | 27.4 | 48.7 | 21.2 | 23.2 | 77.5 | 57.3 |
| 1920 .................... | 35.4 | 53.3 | 27.0 | 28.5 | 84.3 | 61.6 |
| 1930 .................... | 43.7 | 57.6 | 31.7 | 35.0 | 88.1 | 65.5 |
| 1940 .................... | 48.6 | 59.0 | 36.5 | 36.8 | 89.1 | 67.4 |
| 1950 .................... | 62.4 | 64.3 | 47.7 | 48.9 | 93.5 | 70.1 |
| 1960 .................... | 73.2 | 69.6 | 58.4 | 58.6 | 95.3 | 73.7 |

SOURCES: *1920-40: Sixteenth Census of the United States: 1940 Population, Vol. II, Characteristics of the Population,* Pts. 1-7, tables 4, 5 for each State (U. S. Bureau of the Census).
*1950: Census of Population, 1950, Vol. II, Characteristics of the Population,* Pt. 1, United States Summary, table 145 (U. S. Bureau of the Census).
*1960: Census of Population, Detailed Characteristics, United States Summary* Final Report PC(1)1D, tables 158, 233; 1910: *Abstract of the Thirteenth Census* (1910), table 28, p. 103 (U. S. Bureau of the Census).

immigrant doesn't have the same political opportunities to achieve economic ends. In addition to the political results of gerrymandering, the city machine has been crumbling for a long time. This is partly the result of past reforms. Civil Service at every level of government now controls many jobs. When a Negro, for instance, was a New York City borough president he was able to dole out only a few jobs. In addition, the machine, as Raymond Mack has pointed out, is breaking down for other reasons: the decentralization of metropolitan centers, the growth of suburbs and satellite towns, the rise of functional groups, and the increasing middle-class character of American life. Despite the growing concentration of Negroes in our large Northern cities, therefore, the old opportunities for jobs which earlier immigrants found immediately available—as well as the opportunities for advancement—no longer exist. But prejudice and the cumulative results of the peculiarities of the Negro American's history remains.

One result of this is the high Negro unemployment rate which has been twice that

TABLE IV

AREA OF BIRTH OF THE NONWHITE POPULATION IN THE NORTHERN[1] AND WESTERN CITIES OF GREATEST NEGRO CONCENTRATION, BY CITY OF RESIDENCE, 1960

| | 1960 population | | | Percent distribution | | |
|---|---|---|---|---|---|---|
| City | Negro[2] | Native non-white[3] | Total native non-white[3] | Born in State or region of 1960 residence | Born in South | Born in remaining regions or other[4] area |
| New York | 1,084,862 | 1,045,626 | 100.0 | 49.0 | 39.2 | 11.8 |
| Chicago | 812,836 | 828,253 | 100.0 | 41.6 | 44.1 | 14.3 |
| Philadelphia[5] | 529,191 | 530,539 | 100.0 | 52.5 | 39.6 | 7.9 |
| Detroit | 482,260 | 483,168 | 100.0 | 44.5 | 48.0 | 7.5 |
| Washington, D.C. | 411,612 | 413,110 | 100.0 | 44.4 | 43.0 | 12.6 |
| Los Angeles | 334,763 | 392,866 | 100.0 | 38.7 | 45.6 | 15.7 |
| Cleveland | 250,889 | 251,693 | 100.0 | 44.5 | 47.8 | 7.7 |
| St. Louis | 214,174 | 215,528 | 100.0 | 51.6 | 39.9 | 8.5 |
| Newark | 137,467 | 137,949 | 100.0 | 46.1 | 43.3 | 10.6 |
| Cincinnati | 108,502 | 109,029 | 100.0 | 51.9 | 40.8 | 7.3 |

[4]Washington, D.C., included
[2]Includes small proportion of Negro immigrants from other countries. This column is shown to illustrate the close conformance in these cities between the Negro and nonwhite population.
[3]Includes native born Negroes, Indians, Japanese, Chinese, and Filipinos.
[4]Includes regions other than present region of residence and south, U.S. outlying areas, born abroad or at sea, and not reported.
[5]County.
[6]Proportion born in Washington, D.C.

SOURCE: *Census of Population, 1960, Detailed Characteristics,* for each State represented, tables 96 and 98 (U. S. Bureau of the Census).

of the white rate since 1957 (see Table V). In the spring of 1966, national unemployment was at its lowest level in 12 years and Negroes accounted for more than 20 percent of the unemployed and 25 percent of the long-term jobless, even though Negroes are only 11 percent of the work force.

The national Negro unemployment situation is bad, and that of the ghettos is worse and getting worse. In Watts, the unemployment rate for most of 1966 was nearly as high as it was in Watts during the recession year of 1960 — 13 percent. There was a sharp rise in the proportion of men who have dropped out of the labor force (that is, they stopped working or looking for work) during the last years. In 1960, about 70 percent of men in Watts were in the labor force, as compared with only 58 percent in 1965.

Herman Miller of the Census Bureau reported in May, 1966:

> "the economic status of Negroes (in Watts) has deteriorated in the past five years in sharp contrast to the experience of the nation as a whole. In Watts and similar Negro neighborhoods, around Los Angeles, family income has declined, the number of poor people has risen, housing has deteriorated, there has been no improvement in unemployment and no change in the job opportunities available to Negroes."[25]

40

TABLE V

Unemployment Rates, %

| | 1930 | 1940 | 1950 | 1957 | 1958 | 1959 | 1960 | 1961 | 1962 | 1963 | 1964 |
|---|---|---|---|---|---|---|---|---|---|---|---|
| White | 6.6 | 14.1 | 4.5 | 3.9 | 6.1 | 4.9 | 5.0 | 6.0 | 4.9 | 5.1 | 4.6 |
| Nonwhite | 6.1 | 16.9 | 7.9 | 8.0 | 12.6 | 10.7 | 10.2 | 12.5 | 11.0 | 10.9 | 9.8 |

SOURCE: *Daniel Patrick Maynihan, Employment, Income and the Negro Family,* The Negro American, (Cambridge, Mass., 1966). p. 137-139

Employment figures don't tell the whole story. In 1964, the rate at which unemployed Negroes had involuntarily lost their jobs (as distinct from the rate of unemployment for all reasons) was at least two and one-half times that of unemployed whites. Furthermore, nearly half of all Negroes in the labor force are laborers, janitors, porters, busboys, or dishwashers. (See Table VI). As a matter of fact, the 1960 occupational structure of Negro males was similar to that for white males of 60 years ago — a fact of little comfort to those groups and individuals concerned about the status of the American Negro. Finally, people who have low jobs or none at all can't earn much money.

*Median Family Income*

| | White | Non-white |
|---|---|---|
| 1947 . . . . . | $3,157 | $1,614 |
| 1950 . . . . . | 3,445 | 1,869 |
| 1960 . . . . . | 5,835 | 3,233 |
| 1963 . . . . . | 6,548 | 3,465 |
| 1964 . . . . . | 6,848 | 3,839 |

Statistical Abstract. U.S. Bureau of the Census (Washington, D.C., 1966) p. 339

TABLE VI

| Occupation Group | Negro | Chinese | Japanese | White |
|---|---|---|---|---|
| | | *1960* | | |
| All occupations | 100 | 100 | 100 | 100 |
| Professional, managerial, clerical, trade | 15.3 | 47.3 | 56.7 | 42.6 |
| Farmers | 4.3 | .7 | 17.1 | 5.6 |
| Craftsmen | 34.2 | 17.6 | 20.1 | 40.0 |
| Laborers & service | 42.1 | 28.0 | 18.5 | 13.2 |
| Unknown | 8.4 | 7.1 | 4.8 | 4.2 |
| | | *1950* | | |
| Professional, etc. | 21.6 | 41.1 | 39.4 | 43.1 |
| Farmers | 13.3 | 1.4 | 15.3 | 10.0 |
| Craftsmen | 28.8 | 19.8 | 17.4 | 39.7 |
| Laborers & service | 48.5 | 37.8 | 42.1 | 16.0 |
| Unknown | 1.5 | 1.3 | 1.1 | 1.1 |

Source: Census of Population, 1950, Vol. II, Pt. I. U. S. Summary, Table 159 and Vol. IV, Special Reports, Pt. 3, Ch. B, Nonwhite Population by Race, tables 11, 12, and Census of Population, 1960, Detailed Characteristics, U. S. Summary, Final Report PC (1)-(1)D, table 205, and Subject Reports, Nonwhite Population by Race, PC (2)-1C, tables 39, 40 (U. S. Bureau of the Census)

The following table puts it another way. (To read: in 1949 non-white family median income was 51.1 percent of white family median income)

*Ratio of nonwhite to white family median income in the United States:*

| | | | |
|---|---|---|---|
| 1949 .... 51.1 | 1953 .... 56.5 | 1957 .... 53.8 |
| 1950 .... 53.9 | 1954 .... 55.6 | 1958 .... 51.4 |
| 1951 .... 52.9 | 1955 .... 55.6 | 1959 .... 51.6 |
| 1952 .... 57.0 | 1956 .... 52.9 | 1960 .... 55.4 |

SOURCE: *Trends in the Income of Families and Persons in the United States: 1947 to 1960 Technical Paper 8, table 9* (U.S. Bureau of the Census)

This is not to say that Negroes have not made progress. Negroes have made great progress in the professional fields. But these accomplishments do not mean the difficulties of the average Negro in finding a job have ended.

While the number of Negroes holding jobs climbed from 6.4 million in 1955 to 7.7 million in 1965, raising their ratio from 10.2 to 10.7 percent of the total work force, Negro joblessness actually rose in that period while white unemployment declined. And joblessness among Negro teenagers has continued at exceedingly high levels.

The most severe problem is among the young Negro and even after he finally gets into the work force the type of job he gets, as indicated in Table VI, is of the blue-collar, lower paying variety. In the past, the political machine, the church, fraternal organization, or labor union, offered some hope and incentive for the immigrant. Not only that, but a cold-hearted laissez-faire society forced the immigrants and the institutions representing them to "root, hog, or die." The social pressure on the modern Negro immigrant is quite different. Let me briefly elaborate.

The welfare programs, Irving Kristol has pointed out, make a serious drain on the ghetto's capacity to develop itself. That is, he says, "the more money we spend on public welfare, and the easier we make it for people to qualify for public welfare, the more people we can expect to find on welfare."[28] This does not mean (nor does Kristol favor) that there should be any reductions in welfare expenditures. But, comparing the ghetto with the immigrants 50-100 years ago, one must very frankly and candidly observe that the liberation of our modern poor by an enlightened and humanitarian social philosophy from the ravages of the economic jungle has also had the effect of dampening natural forces within the ghetto for self-development.

Glazer and Moynihan pointed out that the immigrants of other ethnic groups took as their models those members of their own groups who attained economic success or public prestige in the city. But today the following report from Cleveland is all to accurate for every neighborhood in our Negro ghettos:

> "Ask any Negro living in the low-income neighborhoods whom they admire as successful stars in their communities.
> They don't name leaders of the NAACP or their councilmen or ministers. They name men who made Easy Street off the rackets. . . .
> To them the numbers and policy game rackets were the only ways open for Negroes to make big money quickly."[27]

To change this we must first change the ghetto from a welfare society to an achieving society.

To do this there must be the motivation to achieve.

In his monumental book, The Achieving Society, David McClelland, Chairman of the Department of Social Relations, Howard University, demonstrates the direct relationship between achievement motivation and economic development.[28/] By achievement motivation he means the internal psychological drive or need to achieve. The classic demonstration is Max Weber's "Protestantism and the Rise of Capitalism" where Weber describes how the Protestant Reformation produced a new character type which infused a more vigorous spirit into the attitude of both workers and entrepeneurs and which ultimately resulted in the development of modern industrial capitalism. McClelland interprets Weber's argument in terms of a revolution in the family, leading to more sons with strong internalized achievement drives. Using modern psychological, empirical methods, McClelland measures the achievement drive or the need for achievement in various civilizations as well as different ethnic and religious groups. He has discovered that "Negroes as a group are significantly lower than practically all the other groups tested" in the need for achievement but he also has found that "middle and upper class Negroes are conspicuously high . . . reflecting once again the fact that individuals who have managed to move out of a low achievement (need for achievement) group tend to have exceptionally high achievement."[29] This points directly, then, at the Negro family.

Pat Moynihan and others have made a major contribution to our understanding of ghetto residents by their analyses of Negro family life. The family is the initial point of entry of an individual into society. In addition to providing emotional security for the individual, it develops a common set of motives which prepare, or should prepare, the child to live comfortably and productively in the various positions that society offers.

> "Among the capacities the family is supposed to initiate and develop are: A system of specific language, arithmetic, and time symbols; general information about the where, what, and how of things our culture values; a set of interpersonal skills by which one protects his own interests, and maintains stable and satifying relations with sub-ordinates, peers, and superiors; and, finally, ways of thinking, feeling, and working for things which characterize each person's individual style of life. By now the evidence is rapidly mounting that the socialization of certain individuals is defective, that one source of the defections lies within the family, and that these defective products are not equally distributed among all social or ethnic groups.[30]

There is also mounting evidence that men raised in mother-centered families lack a suitable role model from whom to learn how to achieve various middle class goals. That is, it is very hard lacking other models to introduce the world of work to a young man who never had in his childhood a steadily working father.

Moynihan has discovered that nearly a quarter of Negro women living in cities who have ever married are divorced, separated, or living apart from their husbands. Almost one-quarter of non-white families are headed by a woman and at any given moment some 36 percent of Negro children are living in homes where one or both parents are missing. This probably means that not much more than one-third of Negro youth reach eighteen having lived all their lives with both their parents.[31/]

One result of this broken family structure in Negro communities is the low level of achievement by Negro students as compared to white students.)The Coleman Report on "Equality of Educational Opportunity" discovered this but it also, most significantly, learned that *"if a minority pupil from a home without much educational strength is put with schoolmates with strong educational backgrounds, his achievement is likely to rise."*[32/] (Underlines supplied) In other words,( achievement motivation can be induced by an environment of success symobls) McClelland has separately made the same discovery.[33/]

This cannot be over-emphasized for understanding this provides us with the means of breaking the vicious circle of poverty breeding poverty, apathy breeding apathy, frustration breeding greater frustration. (What this means is that what is desperately needed in the ghetto is the creation of success symbols, at the neighborhood and block level, inducing a sense of locally recognized accomplishment and leading thereby to black pride, Negro self-respect and the achieving ghetto. In the American culture, this means jobs.)

Jobs are the great need in a land where people are judged by what they do, by what they get done, and by how much they accumulate. I do not say that jobs are the sole solution to the ghetto problem, but I do insist most emphatically that unless jobs are provided for the Negro youth soon, jobs of security, jobs with career possibilities — not leaf raking or make-work type labor — jobs that any other American who does not go on to college seeks and finds, unless these jobs are provided for Negroes, all the education and training programs are practically futile.) As Senator Robert Kennedy (D., N.Y.) has said:

"Employment is the only true long-run solution; only if Negroes achieve full and equal

48

employment will they be able to support themselves and their families, become active citizens
and not passive objects of our action, become
contributing members and not recipients of
our charity. This is not to say that education,
for example, is not critical to future employment and self-sufficiency; of course, it is. But
it is to say that unless we achieve employment,
by whatever means or programs, we will never
solve the problem. People with jobs can buy
or rent their own housing; people with adequate incomes can see that their children are
educated; people with jobs can mark out their
own relationships with their fellows of whatever color. But without employment, without
basic economic security and self-sufficiency,
any other help we provide will be only tem-
porary in effect."[34/]

Bayard Rustin has succinctly stated the need
for jobs better than anyone:

"In this society one's spiritual judgment of
himself has . . . to be related to his role in the production of goods and services. He is someone
because he does something which society puts
a value upon."[35/]

Our top governmental policy makers and the
majority of academicians, in their olympian
indifference to the motivational factors of
individual as well as community behavior,
have erred grievously in failing to appreciate
the all-important significance of jobs to Negroes.

It is my view that we have been kidding ourselves too long with our Federal programs by

presuming education and other "long-run" programs are the only solutions to the ghetto. There is a deeper instinct involved that runs with time "We must needs do," Padraic Pearse said, "we must needs create." This is true for all of us, particularly in this country, and more particularly for a group that is trying to prove itself in its own way, at this time.

How many riots in how many cities do we need in this country to sink the point home that our programs for the ghetto cannot all be aimed in the long run? We are in grave danger in this country, I strongly believe, of permitting the development of a generation of young Negroes who will continue for the rest of their lives bitter, prone to violence, and hateful of all things white — and for good reason. The Negro's sounds of NOW are not irrational demands or threats; they are a cry of desperation; a plea for opportunity and one last lamentation for understanding and justice.

The San Francisco riot of September, 1966 as reported in the San Francisco Chronicle of September 29, 1966, makes this very clear:

> "Mayor John F. Shelley pleaded desperately with President Johnson and other Federal Officials last night for emergency funds to attack the 'critical unemployment situation' among the city Negroes.
>
> "The Mayor cited the jobless situation facing young Negroes here — at least one in four is

unable to find work — as the chief cause of the current racial rioting."

"What did jobs do during World War II?" Surely economists are not so limited by their discipline that they do not appreciate the motivational and thus economic consequences of the social conditions existing during World War II. Negroes could not attend a public restaurant, theatre or public park; they rode in the back of the bus; were universally treated with contempt; were not admitted to churches; their educational opportunities were almost nil. We have made great progress in these areas in the last twenty years. Now that the Negro has the encouragement of full citizenship and is at the verge of expanding his personality if given the opportunity, we are told that jobs are no solution.

If we expect the Negro to contribute significantly to the development of the ghetto, as the vast majority of Negroes prefer, we had better do something about the job problem *now* or brace ourselves to a frustrated and bitter generation of Negroes.

# CHAPTER 2
# JOBS FOR THE GHETTO

"You know the average young person out here
don't have a job, man, they don't have anything
to do. They don't have any alternative, you know,
but to go out there and try to make a living for
themselves. Like when you come down to the
Tombs down there, they're down there for rob-
bing and breaking in. They want to know why
you did it and where you live, but you have to
live. You go down to the employment agency
and you can't get a job. They have you waiting
all day, but you can't get a job. They don't have
a job for you. You have to live. I'm ready to do
anything anyone else is ready to do—because I
want to live—I want to live. No one wants to
die. I want to live."1/

It is indefensible that the Poverty Program,
with all due respect to Sargent Shriver, its dedicated and tireless director, has never really
come directly to grips with the job problem.
The Poverty Program, as originally conceived,
was to raise the level of income of those in poverty by providing better jobs. But somewhere

53

along the line in the drafting stages it was decided that the poor must be pre-conditioned for work and responsibility. The program, now locked eternally in its original legislative package, has ever since been rich on programs for the intellectual elite and poor on jobs for the poor.) As Milton Kother of the Institute for Policy Studies has observed, (and Moynihan has made a similar point):

> "Headstart assumed poor education as a root cause of poverty; manpower training programs assumed inadequate skills as a root cause; community action assumed powerlessness as a root cause, and so on. . . all of these root causes were united toward a common aim: employment. The only difficulty was that by and large no major employment issued from their various programs. No substantial employment market outside the ghetto seemed to await the remedied clients of poverty."2/

I agree with Herbert Hill, labor secretary of the NAACP, who said:

> 'The historic civil rights gains won by Negroes in the last twenty years are in danger of being destroyed by the growing crisis of unemployment and underemployment that directly affects the well-being of the entire Negro Community and that leads to acute social dislocation and despair. This has the gravest implication for the whole of American society."3/

It is argued that the better paying jobs unemployed Negroes may be trainable for are going out of style. In fact, it has become almost

54

intellectually fashionable in recent years to predict all sorts of dire, dramatic changes to be brought about very suddenly by automation, including the virtual elimination of the blue collar job. This is nonsense, Charles Silberman points out, "Automation is not a significant cause of unemployment, in large part because there isn't much automation." The myth-makers, he says, "fail to distinguish between what is scientifically possible and what is economically feasible."[4] Silberman quotes Albert Wahlstetter, the mathematical logician, to the effect that technological change "has to do with such grubby matters as costs," and he refers to Joseph Schumpeter's frequent argument that invention played a relatively minor role in technological change. What was crucial, Schumpeter insisted, was "innovation" — the process of finding economic applications for the inventions.[5]

"New technology," Silberman asserts, "is exerting far less impact than had been assumed on the kinds of work men do and the amount of education and skill they need to do it."[6] Employment of manufacturing production workers increased by one million in the three and a half years from the first quarter of 1961 to the third quarter of 1964 and by another 700,000 by the fourth quarter of 1965. In short, Silberman concludes that it's more than likely that as long as the national economy remains strong there will be a growing demand for manufacturing production workers.[7]

I expressed the view in Chapter I that the ghetto is here to stay for a long time. Any job program for Negroes must confront this fact. The ghetto's problems, in turn, must be viewed within the context of the problems of the city.

It is obvious to all what has been going on in almost every major northern American city. The middle class and upper class whites are moving out; Negroes are moving in. For example, between 1950 and 1960, Chicago's central city experienced a net loss of 399,000 whites and a net gain of 320,000 Negroes; Detroit lost 363,000 whites and gained 182,000 Negroes; New York lost 476,000 whites and gained 240,000 Negroes. At the same time this is happening, the industrial jobs are moving to the suburbs. New York lost 204,000 industrial jobs between 1947 and 1964. Between 1960 and 1964 alone, New York lost 8.2 percent of its manufacturing jobs; Philadelphia lost 4 percent; and Pittsburgh lost 5 percent.[8]

The result, of course, is that the unemployment rate for Negroes is going up, the demand for city services is increasing, and the tax resources with which to pay them is decreasing.

According to the 1960 census, 25 percent of the immigrants into New York City during the previous five years had annual family incomes below $4,000, while only 6½ percent of those who had moved from the city to neighboring suburbs were in that category. And over the years, the First National City Bank's economic survey indicates, "the personal income base has been rising much more slowly than municipal expenditures."[9] The City's expense budget was $4½ billion for fiscal year 1967 which was double the budget seven years earlier. The Bank's study comments that it is difficult to envisage how "American cities can continue receiving a minor share of overall governmental revenues while being called upon to assume the increasing burdens resulting from population shifts which are nation-wide in their genesis and scope."[10]

This state of affairs not only will continue unless serious efforts are made to overcome it, but more than likely will get worse — very seriously worse. This is the conclusion of a brilliant young economist, whom I was fortunate to have as an assistant in the U. S. Department of Commerce, Dr. Martin McGuire.

McGuire and his associates completed in December, 1966, the most detailed projections of unemployment and population migration patterns for the period of fiscal year 1967 to fiscal year 1975 that have ever been made for any comparable period of time. Among other things, McGuire's analysis shows that over this period the natural rate of increase of population and labor force in America's biggest cities will be greater than the rate of growth of job opportunities in those cities. More particularly, the source of the job shortage problem is in the central cities. Abstracting from California, which is a special case, even if all the labor force absorbed by expanding job opportunities in the suburban and outer-ring counties of the 29 largest metropolitan areas comes from their Central Cities, McGuire estimates that by 1975 9.8% of this population still must either migrate to smaller counties outside the metropolitan areas or find jobs at home. This 9.8% is an enormous figure in absolute numbers, i.e., 7.1 million people or 2.9 million jobs. "It seems extremely unlikely," McGuire notes, "that that number of people, many of them Negroes, can or will reverse the migration trends of the decade 1950-1960 and leave the cities."[11/]

The Center for Research in Marketing, Peekskill, N. Y. estimates that by 1970 Negroes will constitute the following percentages of the cities listed:

| | | |
|---|---|---|
| a) | Baltimore | 47% |
| b) | Chicago | 32% |
| c) | Cleveland | 38% |
| d) | Detroit | 47% |
| e) | Los Angeles | 23% |

| f) | Miami | 28% |
| g) | New Orleans | 45% |
| h) | New York City | 19% |
| i) | Philadelphia | 32% |
| j) | St. Louis | 46% |
| k) | Washington, D.C. | 68% |

The "traffickists", as Victor Gruen, the noted architect and planner, calls the group of experts who would solve city problems almost exclusively through improved transportation methods, will no doubt disagree with the idea of bringing jobs to the city. While acknowledging that improved transportation is needed and would be helpful I agree with McGuire that the problem of excess labor in the Central Cities will be so large measured in absolute numbers that it cannot be solved simply by improving commuting patterns. Furthermore, the costs required to solve the problem even if improved transportation methods alone were the answer would not only be fairly astronomical but would make the city a mere function of the transportation department at just the time the humanist feelings of America are trying to make the city a beautiful and fit place to live. Finally, for the reasons mentioned in Chapter 1, Negroes will continue to live near each other in very large numbers for a long time to come. This is the heart of the problem. Ways must be developed to create jobs in the city that the unemployed and underemployed residents of the city, growing more and more Negro, can be trained to occupy.

Why have industries been moving out of the city? There are two main reasons: (1) the evolution in transportation technology; and (2) the economies of one-story factories. The advancements in trucking and the consequent development of super highways have had the effect of substituting this mode of transportation for rail into open fringe urban spaces at the expense of the central city space. By arranging production horizontally, manufacturers discovered that they were able to use less labor in a one-story plant than in a multi-story building.

The economics of this post-war trend have been very ably explained in the Mid-Chicago Economic Development Study sponsored by the City of Chicago:

> "Land prices descend in direct relationship to distance from the Central Business District of the City. Confining the discussion only to industrial land, economists have explained this relationship in the following way: Different land prices across the urban space reflect some difference in the 'return' or profit on one piece of land as compared to another. In an urban economy, the difference in price reflects transportation savings available to certain kinds of firms on higher priced land.
>
> Products, services or labor may be moved to 'near in' locations in less time and at less cost than to locations on the metropolitan fringe.

Since 'near in' locations reflect such savings in costs of transportation, different land prices serve to allocate the scarce resource of 'near in' land to companies which will realize the greatest benefits or profits from it.

Thus, the building of expressways and substitution of trucking as a module reduces the transportation savings of 'near in' as opposed to 'fringe' land. Downward pressure was brought to bear on the price of industrial land in the study area while prices on the suburban fringe began to rise. As important as the substitution of cheaper land in the suburbans for more expensive land in the city was the change permitted in production methods resulting from the ability to use lower priced land. By substituting expensive amounts of cheap land, as was pointed out earlier, the industrialist was able to substitute land costs for those of labor and capital.

There is one implication of this principle that deserves special mention. *It is only possible to economically engage in this substitution as long as land costs are low. Suburban land costs have risen considerably in the past five years and are beginning to approach prices in the city. There are certain physical limits as to how far transportation advantages of a metropolitan area can be extended outward before it becomes uneconomic to transport labor, products, and business services. And that limit is approaching rapidly.* Land prices have begun an upward swing across the metropolitan plane, reversing the cycle and reinstating the advantages of the city vis-a-vis the suburban fringe. For industrialists tied to the metropolitan area or the city by markets, suppliers or labor, price rises on land will create incentives to conserve on that factor of production. This should mean the renaissance of the multi-story structure."[12] (Italics added.)

Mayor Lindsay of New York City summarized the changes taking place as far as industry's move to the suburbs in concerned as follows:

> "Fifteen years ago a business could acquire a 30-acre plot in the suburbs and put up a single-story plant. Taxes were negligible. Now, not only is it difficult to find a 30-acre plot—the cost of land is up 500 percent—but the tax gap between city and suburbs is closing.
>
> "Additionally, we have reports from firms that have relocated, detailing difficulties in obtaining an adequate supply of labor. And, of course, their costs of bringing their goods to market have increased."[13/]

In short, while the jobs that Negroes have been most trained to fill or the most trainable to fill have been leaving the city in the postwar era, the Negroes at the same time have been moving into the city with the obvious result there is a drastic rise in the rate of Negro unemployment.

How do we cure Negro unemployment?

We have two options: do something or do nothing. The latter is unthinkable. It would seem obvious that we should do the former, but many people do not think so. These people think we should do nothing because to do anything will accelerate the migration of Southern Negroes to our Northern cities. That argument assumes a perfect job information line, something which does not exist. For the past

70 years, as I pointed out in Chapter I, Southern Negroes have been streaming to Northern and Western areas; they will continue to do so, regardless of whether we try to solve the Negro urban unemployment problem. To do nothing will simply aggravate the problem.

Furthermore, there is no reason why the Federal Government couldn't be more effective in providing jobs for Negroes in the South with existing programs. A plan has been developed that in my opinion is fully practical and effective and has the further virtue of having been tried successfully in practice. This plan could be invoked routinely by any Federal agency involved in a construction, lending, or granting program leading to the employment of people even though increased employment may not be the main objective of the particular Federal activity involved. This requires some explanation in detail in order to illustrate adequately how this plan works in a concrete situation.

The plan referred to, called the Bradford Employment Plan, was developed by Mr. Amory Bradford, formerly General Manager of the N. Y. Times, for the Economic Development Administration (E.D.A.) of the U. S. Department of Commerce in Oakland, California.

Oakland is an industrial city with a population of about 400,000, with many of the problems common to all older central cities. It is well situated with respect to air, water and rail transportation, but much of its industrial plant is obsolete. Since World War II, its middle class white population has moved out to the suburbs, leaving the deteriorating residential areas to the increasing Negro and Mexican-American populations, which now comprise about 40 percent of the total. The unemployment rates of the latter are double that of the white population, and are estimated at between 15 percent and 20 percent.

In January, 1966, when I was serving as Assistant Secretary of Commerce for Economic Development, I met for two days with Oakland's business and municipal leaders to devise a program which would maximize the employment of the local long-term unemployed, in this case mainly Negroes and Mexican-Americans. The E.D.A. committed itself to invest a minimum of $15 million in the industrial development of Oakland for new buildings, renovation, and necessary public facilities, contingent upon the development of a workable and enforceable plan which would obligate the city and those businesses directly benefiting from the E.D.A. investment to train and hire the long-term unemployed. I engaged the services of Bradford to serve as a professional consultant to E.D.A. and to develop such a workable, enforceable plan.

It became immediately apparent to Bradford that it would be extremely difficult to establish a structure to supervise the administration of the program. It was also clear that each employer who expanded employment in Oakland as the result of EDA public works grants or business loans had unique employment patterns which could not easily be regulated by any general directive as to maximum possible employment of the presently unemployed.

Bradford developed a system in which each employer directly benefiting from the E.D.A. investment is asked to draw up an Employment Plan covering his own needs and specifying the categories of skilled and unskilled workers which he would require. The plan shows how the employer proposes to provide maximum employment opportunities for the long-term unemployed residing in the city, including a training program for each skill the employer will need together with his estimates as to the number of long-term unemployed he anticipates can be trained and hired for each skill. These plans are reviewed by an Employment Plan Review Committee which consists of representatives of each of the five Poverty Target Areas, one representative from business, one from labor, and one from EDA. This Committee then reviews the employer's plan and is free to make any comments or recommendations they wish, either individually or as a group. The E.D.A. decides whether or not the Employment Plan justifies a grant or loan; that is, whether or not each plan provides maximum employment opportunities to the hardcore unemployed. Once the grant or loan is approved, the employer is required to file monthly reports. Noncompliance with the plan constitutes a default under the contract entered into with the E.D.A. A binding arbitration provision is included in the contract in order that a skilled industrial relations negotiator can settle any dispute.

The concept of Bradford's Employment Plan was well received by all parties. For the employers it had the desirable feature of flexibility which made it practical since every business has different requirements. Obviously a higher percentage of long-term unemployed could be trained to work in a bakery than in a machine tool shop. For the Negro and Mexican American leaders it offered an active role in reviewing and recommending modifications, if necessary, of the employer's plans according to their knowledge of the community's capabilities, while enabling them to understand the dif-

66

ferent employment needs of each business. The machinery of enforcement was not cumbersome because if minor differences of opinion developed a local committee, including representatives of all interested parties, could work them out. If differences continued for a long period of time or if a major difference developed subsequent to the signing of the contract, legally binding arbitration was provided. The Federal Government, E.D.A., was satisfied because the Plan provides for practical and reasonable flexibility, a method of informed communication to the minority groups, and an enforceable arbritration provision in case of major default.

The E.D.A. subsequently authorized $14,139,000 in public works grants and $9,150,000 in loans for the following projects:

1. Construction of a marine terminal and facilities with improved access roads (Estimated permanent jobs: 430)
2. Construction of new hangar facilities at the airport (Estimated permanent jobs: 1,000)
3. Development and improvement of 30 acres of land for new industrial parks (Estimated permanent jobs: 420)
4. A four-lane roadway facility for vehicular access to the Coliseum complex to permit service, industry, development at the site

of the new Coliseum. (Estimated permanent jobs: 600)

The total number of long-term jobs expected to be created by these expenditures was 2,450 at the outset, with substantial increases in subsequent years. In addition, E.D.A. received 12 applications for loans to businesses, which would provide an additional 800 new jobs.

The effectiveness of Bradford's Employment Plan was soon discovered. Two businesses applied for E.D.A. loans. One applicant agreed to an Employment Plan provision, the other did not. The first applicant received the loan, the second was refused. After four weeks of unsuccessfully finding private financing, the second applicant returned to the E.D.A. and agreed to an Employment Plan.

In brief, then, it is proposed that before any Federal grants or loans are made to a community which would result in permanent employment, an employment plan would be worked out which sought to maximize the training and employment of the local, long-term unemployed along the lines outlined above. In the South for the most part these are Negroes. This would be agreed to by the community which receives the aid as well as the individual businesses or private groups which would directly benefit thereby. Once a plan was reviewed by a local committee, consisting of a majority of "poverty" representatives, and approved by the Federal agency, the company would file a monthly report with the Review Committee and the Agency advising them as to progress toward achieving the objective stated in the plan. In the event of an alleged failure to fulfill the plan, a legally binding arbitration would be provided.

I do not claim that the employment plan concept is the one and final solution to the employment of the Negroes in the South. It is a promising beginning. However, all the other Federal programs that I shall mention in Chapter III for the city can be made equally available to Southern areas, rural and urban. What is needed is a strategy and some determination in both Northern areas as well as Southern areas to link the training and employment of the long-term unemployed with Federal investments.

If jobs are needed in the city for ghetto residents and financing schemes can be developed (as I explain in the next chapter), the obvious question is: where are these jobs going to be located?

Before the question is answered I must make two preliminary observations.

First, despite the serious declines in manufacturing employment in our major cities in recent years there still remains considerable industrial employment in the cities. For instance, the manufacturing employment, numbered in thousands, for the year 1964 stood at the figures indicated for the following cities:[14]

| | | |
|---|---|---|
| a) | New York | 868.7 |
| b) | Chicago | 864.8 |
| c) | Philadelphia | 531.4 |
| d) | Detroit | 522.3 |
| e) | Los Angeles | 748.2 |
| f) | Cleveland | 282.5 |
| g) | St. Louis | 268.1 |
| h) | Newark | 236.1 |
| i) | Cincinnati | 147.9 |
| j) | Pittsburgh | 278.0 |

Second, the continual decline in manufacturing employment not only can be arrested but greatly increased if city planning would be enlarged to include "economic development planning"; i.e., planning to allocate scarce land and other city resources for the purpose of expanding economic opportunities for city residents as well as increasing city revenues. In the past, city planning has been primarily "physical planning", that is, it has been preoccupied with the construction of housing, government facilities and services, and transportation systems.

Let me hasten to add that the mere addition of economic development planning to city planning is totally inadequate for the present day. A city must serve a number of functions which it must bear in mind when allocating its limited land resources. Among other things, it must provide a place for people to live, to work, to get educated, to purchase essential goods and services, to worship, to find recreation and creative opportunities, and to transport themselves between these places. In addition, the city considered as a totality should be edifying and stimulating in its buildings and physical layout.

Heretofore, as I have indicated, city planning has not been comprehensive. But, there have been a few city planners that have sought to consider the city as a whole. These have been primarily brilliant architects who view the city as potentially a thing of beauty. Perhaps their idealistic schemes were too far in advance for a materialistic culture but perhaps also, in many cases, form failed to follow function. In other words, these architects may well have been somewhat contributorily negligent in the poor reception they have had in city planning departments because their plans were somewhat impractical. Not all is lost. The new Model Cities program of the Department of Housing and Urban Development (H.U.D.) could be a big help in bringing traditional city planning and some of the more advanced city planners together. But these latter must bear in mind that the Model Cities program is not speaking to Reston but to Harlem.

The Model Cities program is designed to develop a "total attack" on the social and physical problems in slum and blighted neighborhoods. This means a comprehensive effort to mobilize all available resources to rebuild and revitalize the environment of blighted neighborhoods and improve significantly the lives of the people living in them. The Department of Housing and Urban Development (HUD) will pay 80 percent of the cost of planning and administering the comprehensive programs. In addition, it will provide up to 80 percent of the total non-federal contributions required for all projects or activities assisted by Federal grant-in-aid programs which are carried out as part of a comprehensive, planned program. If the Model Cities program really intends to develop a "total attack" on slum neighborhoods then it must think much broader than city planning traditionally has thought in the past.

Fortunately, some fairly realistic plans have been developed by distinguished architects to aid those cities which are capable of thinking and acting boldly. (And to live on the new frontier of a great society, we need bold minds and bolder hearts.)

The New York Museum of Modern Art commissioned four teams of university architects and city planners in 1966 to show how four fundamental problems of city planning could be imaginatively solved. The area for all four designs included most of Harlem. The two most practical schemes were those developed by M.I.T. and Columbia University.

The M.I.T. plan showed how large segments of underused or misused land could be utilized. It chose the area below the Triborough Bridge, along East River, for its demonstration. There is enough landfill potential here to connect two neighboring islands with each other and with Manhattan. Inside this land-fill, the M.I.T. plan would create a lake purified for boating and swimming. On part of the land-fill would be a new town for 14,000 families. This would still leave 240 acres of a delightful park alongside Harlem. The cost, M.I.T. claims, for earth moving, changing roads and water purification would be approximately $15 million. The beauty of this scheme is that it would provide Harlem with new housing and new opportunities of all kinds without demolishing a single building or displacing a single family.

The Columbia University scheme takes advantage of the air-rights over the elevated railroad which runs from 97th St. to 134th St. This scheme envisages building a concrete vault over the railroad no wider than the existing street. On top and along the sloping sides of this would be housing, shops, and industrial and community facilities. The train would continue to run as a subway. This linear structure has the great advantage that it could be built in stages to permit people living in the path of construction to be re-housed in completed portions as the vault advanced. Columbia estimates that the entire vault and a substantial part of the housing could be put in place in less than two years.

Buckminster Fuller has published a plan in which twice the population of present day Harlem could be placed in 14 conical buildings, providing not only modern living accommodations for all the residents but also freeing scarce land for parks, industry, and other purposes. The City of Chicago is contemplating the construction of a major airport in Lake Michigan several miles from downtown and connected by a tunnel to the central area.

The point of all this is to indicate that it is within our capability to rebuild our cities rationally, by design, to accommodate the various needs, values, and aspirations of the city, if we have the mind and heart to do it.

Understanding, therefore, that I fully appreciate the allocation of a city's land resources must contemplate more than industrial and commercial purposes and that to the extent land resources are allocated for such purposes they should fit within a comprehensive plan that encompasses all of the needs and aspirations of a city, or section of a city, and that the plan must be both pragmatic in meeting needs and humanist in representing values, the following observations offer a number of possibilities for the location of industrial, commercial and service jobs in the city and more particularly in the ghetto.

To begin with, there are vast tracts of land in our major American cities that can be utilized for economic development. The ghetto areas, themselves, are ideally situated for any city's future growth. Look at Harlem, for instance, the way William R. Hudgins does as president of the predominantly Negro-owned Freedom National Bank in Harlem:

> "We have bridges connecting Harlem to Queens and New Jersey. We're serviced by both the East and West Side highways; we have several bus routes, four subway lines and a New York Central Railroad station. Harlem has more potential for growth than any place in New York."[15]

The ghetto has many advantages: large labor market close by; proximity to downtown and its business, financial, engineering, and other services; access to distribution centers and markets; very little local opposition to rebuilding or to industrial development; and generally lower real estate values compared to downtown or suburban industrial property.

Besides ghetto areas, there are large tracts such as the Chicago Stockyards, which once was the site of 30,000 jobs, that could be used for industrial purposes. The Flatland section of Brooklyn, a 100 acre site, has been designated for industrial development. The Brooklyn Navy Yard, an extremely valuable 350 acre location, is being converted into an industrial park to employ three times as many people as the old Navy Yard. Military bases that are being phased out in other cities could be similarly converted.

The Southern and Pacific Railway has highly valuable industrial property in Watts. Hunter's Point in San Francisco has vacant land that could easily be utilized for economic development. The City of Philadelphia, Pennsylvania, reclaimed a large part of its 3,000 acre redevelopment project within the city limits by means of dredging and filling from the Delaware River. Everett, Washington did much the same with 1,500 acres of tidelands. Finally, following the Columbia University design mentioned above, there is the possibility of leasing air rights—space above city-owned garages, freeways, cemeteries, and railroad tracks—for a variety of municipal functions. This should include, among other things, industrial development.

The job potential of all these areas can be maximized in many cases by the development of multi-story industrial buildings and, where feasible, the construction of underground factories.

The Mid-Chicago Economic Development Study, previously referred to, observes:

> "To re-think the multi-story building in terms of its benefits for industry today — and its larger role in area redevelopment — it is essential that one depart from older concepts of such structures as gaunt, dark, and awkward places, bereft of such functional necessities as adequate power and vertical transportation."[16]

The Chicago study includes three basic designs for multi-story buildings from two to ten stories with a technical description of their design as well as their economies. Appendix — contains technical material from the Chicago study demonstrating the feasibility of multi-story plants. Suffice it to say here that the postwar trend of one-story plants is no law of nature and that a great deal of work is being done in industrial architecture in the multi-story factory.

The underground plant can also be utilized in many areas. I have personally toured such a factory employing over 300 people within the city limits of Kansas City, Missouri. There are some important economic advantages to this idea: construction costs are one-half to two-

77

thirds of a building enclosing the same space above ground (Engineering New Record, May 18, 1961); absence of vibration, an important feature for fine precision work, elimination of the extra cost for support of overhead cranes and tracks which can be suspended almost anywhere from rigid ceilings; elimination of the problems of outside repair and maintenance; lower heating, air conditioning, and humidity control costs; lower costs of maintaining adequate security for the plant.

As far as industrial psychological problems, the owner of the Kansas City plant told me:

> "There is little difference between working in an underground facility and working in a windowless air conditioned building such as the new A.T.&T. building in New York. It is my understanding from those with whom we have talked on this subject, both here and in Europe, that the psychological problems are confined largely to those who are concerned about the psychological problems."

As a matter of fact, the great Greek city planner, Constantinos Doxiadis, recommends that future factories be built underground. It only seems strange because it is different and new.

A valuable source of potential jobs for ghetto residents lies in the construction of public buildings as well as in the providing of public services. First, a short digression on integration. I do not believe the white liberal fully realizes how blindly arrogant he can be by

78

presuming that integration is, so to speak, a one-way street; viz., Negroes moving to cozy white suburbs. Why can't integration work the other way around—white people living in or at least working in Negro areas?

This concept of integration could be swiftly advanced by the construction of public buildings in Negro ghettos.) New York State has shown the way in this respect with its announcement that it will construct a $20 million state office building in the heart of Harlem.[17] It will be a 23-story building providing 260,000 square feet of office space, and housing at least 12 state agencies. There are many benefits that will result from this action: new job opportunities close at hand for Harlem residents, an inducement for construction or renovation of other private commercial buildings in the neighborhood, the improvement of real estate values and, consequently, tax revenues, and what I regard as one of the most essential ingredients to any community's development, white or black, a heightened sense of community esprit or morale. This is the old "success breeds success" argument again. Once a community has visible, tangible evidence of significant progress, its spirits and hopes are lifted, its sense of self-esteem, and self-confidence rises, and it finds itself willing and capable of trying and doing more.

79

The opportunities in the next decade for other governmental units to follow New York State's lead are tremendous. There follows a carefully computed estimate made by the Joint Economic Committee of the U. S. Congress with respect to state and local public facility needs during the period of 1966-1975. It is obvious that not all of these facilities could or should be placed in ghettos. But it should be equally obvious that much, much more could be done in this direction as far as ghettos are concerned.

| | | (Dollars in millions) | | |
| | Actual | Estimated | | |
| Type of Facility | 1965 | 1970 | 1975 | 1966-75 |
| --- | --- | --- | --- | --- |
| 1. Area vocational school facilities | NA | 600 | 790 | 6,300 |
| 2. Academic facilities for higher education | 1,525 | 2,250 | 2,960 | 23,500 |
| 3. General hospital facilities | | 1,510 | 1,980 | 15,710 |
| 4. Clinics and other outpatient facilities | 1,926 | 310 | 410 | 3,240 |
| 5. Long-term care facilities | | 600 | 780 | 6,230 |
| 6. Community mental health centers | | 280 | 450 | 2,930 |
| 7. Facilities for the mentally retarded | NA | 330 | 400 | 3,340 |
| 8. Health research facilities | NA | 460 | 600 | 4,800 |
| 9. Medical and other health schools | NA | 690 | 910 | 7,210 |
| 10. Arena, auditoriums, exhibition halls | 667 | 770 | 1,010 | 8,000 |
| 11. Theaters and community art centers | NA | 700 | 910 | 7,230 |
| 12. Museums | 25 | 90 | 120 | 950 |
| 13. Public Libraries | 103 | 190 | 240 | 1,910 |
| 14. Residential group care facilities for children | NA | 80 | 110 | 840 |
| 15. Armories | 1 | 15 | 15 | 145 |
| 16. Fire stations | 191 | 130 | 170 | 1,370 |
| 17. Public office and court buildings | 218 | 320 | 400 | 3,250 |

(State and Local Public Facility Needs and Financing, Volume 1 - P.23, U. S. Government Printing Office)

A rich source of job opportunities also lies in public service employment. The National

Commission on Technology, Automation and Economic Progress, appointed by President Johnson in December, 1964, recommended in its report to him in February, 1966:

"1 — that public service employment opportunities be provided to those unsuccessful in the competition for existing jobs;

"2 — that a 5-year program be established, with the amount of public service em-employment increased each year, depending upon previous experience and labor market conditions;

"3 — that an initial sum of perhaps $2 billion be appropriated to provide about 500,000 additional full-time public service jobs."

The Commission estimated the potential sources of new jobs through public service employment as follows:

| Source of Employment | Job Potential (in millions) |
|---|---|
| Medical institutions and health services | 1.2 |
| Educational institutions | 1.1 |
| National beautification | 1.3 |
| Welfare and home care | 0.7 |
| Public protection | 0.35 |
| Urban renewal and sanitation | 0.65 |
| Total....... | 5.3 |

The Commission's recommendations frankly recognizes the anomaly of excessive unemployment in a society confronted with a huge backlog of public service needs. It notes that employing the unemployed can be almost costless since the unemployed only consume and do not produce.

Much of the work that needs doing requires only limited skills and minor amounts of training. The Economic Development Administration conducted an experiment along this line in Cleveland, Ohio in 1966. It deserves some attention because it not only shows the great possibilities that lie in this field but also the great inertia that must be overcome while trying to work with complacent institutions such as the State Employment Service.

When the E.D.A., stimulated by Representative Charles A. Vanik (D-Ohio), proposed a training and employment program in 1965 for unemployed Cleveland residents in hospital and related occupations, the Ohio State Employment Service found they had "no jobs listed" because the hospitals did not answer their postcard questionnaire and thus "there were no jobs and there could, therefore, be no training programs." The man who had conceived this idea and who was to carry it out (and who was my predecessor as Administrator of the economic development program of the U. S. Department of Commerce), Mr. Bill Batt, had been around the manpower field too long to be put off by this response. Batt went directly to the Cleveland Hospital Council, representing 48 area hospitals, and prevailed upon the Council to make its own job survey. The Hospital Council was astounded to learn that there was an immediate need for 2,000 workers and that this would increase to 3,000 within 18 months. The Council declared itself ready to cooperate on both a training and a placement program.

The State Employment Service was obviously embarrassed by the Council's findings. Like many other old-line, well-entrenched governmental agencies, coasting along from appropriation to appropriation, suddenly held up before a public previously unsuspecting its existence, the State Employment Service immediately proceeded to protect its public record. An officer of the State Employment Service issued a press release stating that "he did not know how he was going to meet this kind of demand—we are scraping the bottom of the barrel in available manpower."

The unemployment rate in just the Hough area (a Negro area) of Cleveland at this time was over 20%.

The Hospital Council thereupon threw up its hands and said it would have to withdraw its commitment to the project. Batt, if he were an ordinary person, would have given up the first time, and if he were just a run-of-the-mill above ordinary person, should have given up this time. Back he went, however, and with that great persuasiveness that belongs only to the completely dedicated and sincere, he was able to get the Hospital Council to go along on a smaller program.

The E.D.A. finally approved and funded a training program at an estimated cost of $2.4 million to train 1,272 persons in 13 selected hospital and related occupations. The training consists of three phases: orientation, institutional or clinical training, and remedial education. Occupations concerned primarily with patient services are conducted in participating hospitals under hospital and Board of Education supervision. Other occupations and the orientation and remedial education programs are handled at the Manpower Training Center operated by the Cleveland Board of Education.

The project got underway on April 11, 1966 and by August 22, 1966 there had been a total of 347 persons enrolled in 17 separate classes, covering 11 project occupations. That is not even close to the 3,000 positions the Hospital

Council found it would be short but it is exactly 347 greater than the Ohio State Employment Service had uncovered in its "vast" files just six months earlier.

It is important to note that although the project was geared to train both men and women, the enrollment has been 93% female. This is extremely important because no job program for the ghettos can be very effective without providing an opportunity for the women who are, too frequently, the bread-winner of the family to obtain meaningful, secure employment.

Creating jobs for residents of the ghetto will have little meaning if those jobs are actually filled by previously trained people who live in other sections of the city. To enable ghetto residents to get these jobs, they must be trained. The McCone report on the Watts riots stated that "the majority of the unemployed in the south central Los Angeles area are unemployable because they lack skill and training."

Negroes are often accused of not wanting the jobs at hand—yardmen, handymen, dishwashers, or delivery boys. Who would? As a young man in Harlem said, "... people are not chaining themselves to posts, ... demonstrations are not being held, ... people are not exposing themselves to dogs and tear gas so they can go on being delivery boys forever."[19] Or as Claude Brown puts it, the ghetto is a living social memory. Negroes are tired of remembering how for generations they took that job as a dishwasher — and ended up washing dishes all their lives. They now demand what all the rest of us demand — a chance to move up.[20] So the most necessary part of any training program is providing the chance to move up.

There are those, of course, who preach that Negroes can't and won't be trained. One is reminded of George Bernard Shaw's observation in the introduction to Man and Superman: "We laugh at the haughty American nation because it makes the Negro clean its boots and then proves the moral and physical inferiority of the Negro by the fact that he is a shoeblack."[21]

Undoubtedly there is a serious motivation problem with respect to Negroes. That is the whole point of this book. Nevertheless, the results to date with Negro trainees in one Federal training program are very encouraging.

In 1965, 34% of the participants in the manpower and development training programs were Negro. Approximately the same proportion (34%) of Negroes left training because of dissatisfaction with the course. In other words, white trainees  dropped out at the same rate as Negro trainees. Furthermore, Negro trainees who completed the training increased their median weekly earnings from $57 per week in the jobs they held before the training program to $70, as compared to a gain of $4 for white trainees, a clear indication that Negroes can be trained and after acquiring skills, are able to bridge the earning gap between themselves and whites.

There is no lack of training programs financed by the Federal Government, but there is a lack of coordination and imagination. The major programs include:

1. Manpower and Development Training Program (MDTA) - In this program, the Labor Department provides funds to State governments which enables the State Employment Services to organize training programs in the localities they select within the State.

2. On-the-Job Training (OJT) - Here, the Labor Department enters into agreements with private employers, approves their training plans, funds part of the training costs directly to employers, and provides a partial subsistence to the trainees.

3. The Job Corps — This is a residential training program conducted in the rural and urban centers funded by the Office of Economic Opportunity (OEO) for out-of-school, out-of-work young men and women between the ages of

16 and 21, and usually operated by public or private agencies under contracts with OEO.

4. The Neighborhood Youth Corps — run by the Labor Department under the poverty program, it provides full and part-time work experience in the trainee's neighborhood and enables him to stay either at school or increase his employability.

5. The Adult Basic Education Program — run by the Department of Health, Education and Welfare under the poverty program, it provides basic education for adults. (This is additional to the MDTA courses, many of which have a basic education component.)

6. The Work Experience Program — the Welfare Administration of the Department of Health, Education and Welfare gives funds to States, counties, and local communities for on-the-job training, basic literary classes, and vocational instruction and counseling.

7. The Vocational Rehabilitation Program — the Department of Health, Education and Welfare provides funds to the States for rehabilitation programs, serving persons with physical, mental or emotional disabilities for vocational training and supportive services,

This is not a complete list of the Federal training programs because it does not include the programs of the Agriculture Department for farmers, the Interior Department for Indians and Eskimos, or the various demonstration grants made by the Office of Economic Opportunity for the purpose of training poor people for various roles such as teacher aides. It also does not include the many State, community and private training programs that exist. For instance, in the City of Chicago the following training programs are in operation:

The YMCA Program for Detached Workers

Sears Jobs for Youth Program

School Dropout Unit, Rehabilitation Service, Cook County

The Double C Program of the Board of Education (Census and Counseling)

The Double E Program of the Board of Education (Education and Employment)

The Double T Program of the Board of Education (Training and Transition)

Guidance and Education Centers, Board of Education

Chicago Boys Club Youth Development Project

Chicago Youth Centers' Program

Job Opportunity Through Better Skills Project (JOBS)

Neighborhood Youth Corps

MDTA Programs (variously sponsored)

Special Project for the Over-age Child, Dunbar Vocational High School (Ford Foundation)

Literacy Program, Cook County

Special Training Programs for Relief Recipients, Cook County, Chicago Urban League and Board of Education

Tutorial Programs, Various Chicago Universities

Mayor's Committee for New Residents

I have heard of a businessman in New York City who complained of being requested by 40 different training programs to hire their candidates.

Apart from the duplication of efforts, the lack of coordination, and the waste of funds associated with such a potpourri of training programs, there are even more serious problems as they relate to the unemployed Negro. First of all, the bureaucracy associated with vocational training is beyond belief even by Federal Government standards. Whether it is a Washington agency or a State agency funded by Washington, little effort is made to redefine jobs. Programs attempt to fill vacancies according to existing definitions, which have historically worked against the inclusion of unemployed Negroes.

Secondly, the state unemployment services are the quintessence of bureaucratic inertia. Not only do they reflect the prejudices of the area but also, more importantly, the special interests of special groups opposing Negro inclusion into the work force.

Finally, and of greatest importance, the most serious objection to the present training programs is that they are not based on a sound realistic partnership with either the job givers or the minority unemployed who most need help. Training programs are based on "job surveys" which usually take months to complete so that the employment data is frequently stale by the time the training begins. We, therefore, have before us and have had for some time the spectacle of a fast moving dynamic economy producing thousands of jobs, industry crying for skills and, despite the millions of dollars appropriated for training annually, pockets of skill shortages and pockets of unemployed residing unhappily side by side.

The state employment services blame the employers for not registering their needs with them; in many cases, true. The employers complain that the State employment offices are not responsive to their needs, that they are more concerned with continuing old, outmoded practices frozen to bureaucratic procedures, than helping them to acquire a labor force that they can use when they need it; and this is also true. Complaints have been made by employers who exhibit pages of advertising calling for workers, indicating that they had registered their needs and, in most cases, calling for skills which the unemployed could acquire in relatively short time periods, but without response by the State Employment Services. In too many cases, they claim, their wishes are disregarded for a variety of unjustifiable reasons and training funds continue to be used for low level service jobs. The Employment Services on the other hand point to unrealistic high job entrance requirements and to the resistance of the employers to take recruits from the employment offices. Perhaps the blame should be shared. It is true that many personnel divisions have been slow to re-evaluate their job entrance requirements (Why a high school diploma for low skilled jobs? What relationship does a diploma really have to a man's manual dexterity?) It is also true that a share of the blame lies with the Employment Service offices and their partner, the vocational education officials, who have burdened themselves with two misconceived attitudes which hinder the development of a constructive program. We refer to:

1) A distrust and resentment of industry's training programs. This is due in part to a feeling that industry's programs constitute an encroachment on the public domain and in part to a fear that industry is not interested in using a man's full ability. Such attitudes con-

stitute a serious obstacle to developing a realistic partnership which would be fruitful to the unemployed and to the community as a whole. It has been estimated that many Employment Offices get less than 30% of the job listings, and those they get are the low-pay semi or unskilled job openings.

Today, many employers are indicating their willingness to accept the unemployed after short training periods which introduce them to the world of work and to the use of tools, claiming that they will continue the training. This frequently meets with complete skepticism on the part of the Employment Service offices claiming that this practice would merely keep newly employed at unskilled jobs. Perhaps this might be true in some cases; I would suspect that it would not be true in most cases, if only because it would be unprofitable. In any case, should this offer not be explored and tried, since, if successful, it would enable many thousands more to be trained and placed with present appropriations?

2) A lack of confidence in the hard-core unemployed, especially the minority unemployed. In the early days of MDTA, '62 '63 and even '64, there was widespread resistance to including the hard-core minority unemployed in training; testing was used as a meth-

od of "screening out". Today the new attitude is "to give them everything" which frequently means keeping an adult in a classroom many months more than is psychologically good or even necessary. Disregarded are the pressures on an adult with dependents to become a wage earner; disregarded also is the psychological need for a man to prove to himself that he can learn the essence of the trade in approximately the same peroid as a white; and disregarded also are the pleas of industry to "give him enough so that he can handle tools and understand industrial discipline, and we will do the rest—we can't wait a year". As one examines the results, in a number of areas around the country, one faces the inescapable fact that this new attitude, well intentioned though it may be, is but the other side of the same coin (distrust and lack of confidence) that kept most of these people out of training in the early years.

It all seems to add up to the fact that after many years of training programs a sensible realistic method responsive to both management's needs and the needs of the unemployed has yet to be developed. What we obviously need are people in the bureaucratic kingdoms who understand the motivational and economic consequences of the desperate and frustrating social conditions Negroes and other minority groups live in.

Fortunately, some modest beginnings have been made; some cities are improving their service and thousands have been trained and placed after training. In a number of areas, management and employment services have improved their relationship to each other and the results can be seen in the types of training and placements. One new and important development is the Bradford Employment Plan, previously mentioned. Another development is the skills center concept developed by Anne Gould of the E.D.A., which enabled some cities to do an outstanding job of training the unemployed and placing them in industrial jobs. Under this concept both management and labor representatives are part of the center's administration and diligent efforts are made from the beginning to guarantee jobs for those successfully completing the courses.

Another development and an outstanding example of self-help is the Opportunities Industrial Center started by the brilliant and bold leadership of Reverend Leon Sullivan, Negro minister from Philadelphia. His training program has been enormously successful and deserves to be given further elaboration.

Reverend Sullivan noted that vocational training in high schools for Negroes was terribly inadequate; children were trained with tools no one had used for years and for occupa-

95

tions that were disappearing. He convinced his congregation and other Negro friends that the Negro community had to do something by itself. He first raised $102,000 by door-to-door canvassing in Negro areas to begin a new training program. He obtained $250,000 in cash and equipment from local businessmen and another $200,000 from the Ford Foundation. The City of Philadelphia gave him a deserted police station to begin the training and he persuaded experienced individuals to donate their time to instruction. Finally, he obtained commitments from businessmen in the area to accept one of his trainees provided he could get the trainee to the point where he could perform the job in question. In other words, there was a guarantee of a job waiting for each participant.

The result of Reverend Sullivan's efforts has been a phenomenal 90% placement rate. And he has brought out those who would not have come near a State Employment Service. Thankfully, the Labor Department and the Office of Economic Opportunity are now contributing to his program not only in Philadelphia but in similar centers which Reverend Sullivan is setting up throughout the country. Perhaps in a few years we might look forward to the State Employment Services and other training programs adapting Reverend Sullivan's methods.

In addition to the ineffectiveness of the various training programs with respect to ghetto residents, another serious obstacle to Negro employment and one getting increasing attention has to do with labor unions. I have already discussed in Chapter I some of the historical antipathy between the immigrants and Negroes and the expression of this antipathy in the early exclusion of Negroes from the Union movement.

At the present those local labor unions practicing discrimination employ one or more of the following methods: the exclusion of Negroes from membership, segregating local unions into separate unions for whites and Negroes, separating seniority lines in collective bargaining agreement, and refusing to admit qualified Negroes into apprenticeship training programs controlled by unions on the basis that they can't pass their written and oral tests.

While it is becoming increasingly popular to attack the union movement for its racial policies, it should be made very clear that almost without exception the industrial unions in the Northern States have had a long liberal history with respect to Negro participation in the union as well as the union activities. Not all of the industrial unions in the Southern States, however, can share that reputation. The main bone of current contention between Negroes

97

and the labor unions has to do with the craft and building trades. Practices differ from city to city and from local to local. There can be no question that at the national level the AFL-CIO leadership has vigorously supported all civil rights programs and civil rights acts. But the fact still remains that the prominent absence of Negroes on many construction projects, the most visible of all union activities, has had the effect of embittering the mass of Negroes against the entire union movement. I would doubt that the present situation can continue for very long. Proposals for change are likely to take one or more of the following directions:

1. The creation of strictly Negro building trades, which will insist on all or a major share of the building trades jobs on construction projects within a ghetto area. Undoubtedly this would cause major jurisdictional disputes and construction stoppages in our major cities.

2. The adoption of a program similar to that recommended by Herbert Hill, labor secretary to the NAACP:

   a. Open Hiring - Only management would determine a worker's competence for employment. Union membership would not be a condition for employment.

b. Contract Compliance. City, county and state governments must not award contracts to construction companies and contractors that use discriminatory union hiring halls or referral lists as the exclusive source of labor supply.

c. Negro Contractors. All governments must make a special effort to award contracts to Negro-owned construction companies as a way of guaranteeing the employment of Negro workers.

d. Elimination of discrimination in apprenticeship training programs. Cities must remove private, i.e., union control of the operation of apprenticeship training programs in the skilled occupations. A system of objective standards must be established as the bases for admission into such programs. Impartial public agencies must determine eligibility for admission.

3. The open confrontation of the federal government's massive construction programs with the building trades. A start was made in this direction in San Francisco in the summer and fall of 1966. All the Federal agencies engaged in construction projects in the San Francisco Bay Area held several meetings together with representatives of church groups. The

purpose of these meetings was to bring to bear the combined purchasing power of the federal agencies and the churches on the building trades to force them to an agreed upon point-by-point program for the elimination of racial discrimination.

4. The implementation very soon of an aggressive integration policy by the national AFL-CIO at the local union level throughout the country. This is the sensible, reasonable course, for the publicity resulting from such a course would pinpoint the pressure on the handful of locals that are resisting change while offering the majority of the building trades an opportunity to display their non-discriminatory policies and to demonstrate the high skills required for many of the crafts. Unless forceful action is taken in the immediate future it is very likely that the next major battleground of the civil rights movement in this country will be fought in the nation's hiring halls.

In summary, a number of points must be kept in mind:

1. Negroes are moving into the city in large numbers, jobs are moving and unemployment and welfare demands are rising and the city's economic resources are diminishing.

2. There is adequate space in every city for industrial and economic development but city planners must be far more imaginative and

comprehensive in their efforts than in the past.

3. Training is essential but a vigorous shake-up of those in charge is long overdue.

4. Negroes below the middle income level will continue to group together and we ought to frankly face up to the fact. This is not being either racist of patronizing. As the distinguished sociologist, Eric Lincoln, himself a Negro, once told me,- "the poor Negro is not just middle class Negro with less money; he is of a considerably different culture." Every ethnic groups has gone through this experience with beneficial results for the individuals in the group because group solidarity reduces the powerlessness of the individual. By focussing our efforts on group pride and the ghetto self-interest, by developing the economic power of enterprising Negroes, by building success symbols at the block level in terms of the prevailing American culture, we stimulate the motivational impulses necessary to create a self achieving ghetto.

5. We are in desperate need for bold leadership at every level of government involved in urban affairs.

# CHAPTER 3

# A MARSHALL PLAN
# FOR THE GHETTO

"In 1947 when President Truman went to the Congress of the United States with his proposal of the Marshall Plan, he asked that we devote 3% of the gross national product for the reconstruction of Europe. I want to ask you today in terms of the freedom budget, can we do anything less for the reconstruction of America than we have already done for the reconstruction of Europe." — A. Philip Randolph.[1]

Three percent of the country's current gross national product (approximately $750 billion) would amount to $44.5 billion. That huge amount of money on top of existing expenditures would make a dramatic impact on American cities. Such figures are truly required if we ever really intend to attack our ghetto problems. But for this amount of money to be spent wisely, the administration of the funds must be made highly flexible, not only to be

103

made adaptable to the peculiarities of local conditions, but also to be free to enlist the creative capacity of America's enterprising thinkers and doers. With all due respect to the Carpenter of Nazareth, I pray that the meek do not inherit the earth, for they have already inherited the government, and that is the trouble. We need bold and imaginative action in each ghetto and we offer inducements to obtain it. If we can devise schemes for a legitimate profit to be made in the ghetto then we will see the vast economic and talent resources of American business begin to apply themselves to the solution of urban problems. This is just beginning, and we ought to lend every effort to encourage it. The problems faced and successfully met by American companies in underdeveloped countries are far more complex and difficult than those posed by American cities. Therefore, I strongly believe that if profit is the price for avoiding bureaucracy, I am not only for it, but for making it a hallowed term.

The following proposals, considered as a package and including the Bradford employment plan discussed in Chapter II as a necessary adjunct to each proposal involving Federal funds, would provide the large amount of funds Mr. Randolph describes as well as the flexibility of American enterprise that would enable the city to expand its economic resources to meet increasing social demands.

## A. DESIGN A LEASE GUARANTY PROGRAM TO ATTRACT PRIVATE CAPITAL TO THE GHETTO

If this country really wants to attack the problems of the ghetto and to make it livable within this generation, then it must somehow commit financial resources far in excess of that currently contemplated. It is generally understood that some scheme must be devised to encourage private captial to help provide these additional resources. To my knowledge, no such detailed program has been developed. There follows a plan developed by myself and Mr. Jay Schwamm, a mortage banker in New York City, which has been discussed with the most reputable and experienced investment institutions in the country and has been declared entirely sound and practical.

The essence of this scheme involves a federal guarantee of private commercial leases. Briefly stated, if a manufacturer were to lease an industrial plant in a ghetto for 15 years, the federal government would guarantee the owner of the building that the lease commitment would be fulfilled. I shall try to be as non-technical as possible in discussing its

105

intricacies and advantages. It will be helpful, for this purpose, to refer to the Small Business Administration (S.B.A.) which I shall describe in greater detail.

The S.B.A. makes loans to businessmen in three ways. First, it makes what is called a direct loan whereby the SBA provides 100% of the money. Secondly, it participates with a local bank in the loan so that the SBA advances 90% of the funds and the local bank 10%. Finally, it guarantees 90% of a loan made by the local bank where the bank supplies 100% of the money and the SBA sets aside 10% as a reserve to cover its 90% guarantee.

For instance, if the SBA were to make a $100,000 direct loan, SBA provides $100,000 immediately. Under a participation arrangement, on a $100,000 loan SBA would allocate $90,000 immediately and a participating bank $10,000. Under the guarantee method, the bank advances $100,000 immediately subject to an SBA 90% guarantee and the SBA reserves $10,000 in the event of future default. It can be seen, that under the latter method of financing, SBA can make many more loans because it has more loan funds available.

Banks do not favor the guarantee arrangement because they are not ordinarily interested in making long-term loans. But if they have a favorite customer or a customer particularly important to the economy of their community, they may enter into a S.B.A. guaranteed loan. What is needed is a guarantee scheme that appeals to the natural long-term investor— namely the insurance companies, health and welfare funds, and pension trusts and which applies to any business, large or small, locating in a ghetto. This could take the form of a loan guarantee without the $350,000 restriction of the SBA or a lease guarantee. I would recommend that either be permitted but that the lease guarantee be encouraged for reasons that shall be described.

Under the lease guarantee proposal, a major insurance company, for instance, would finance the construction of a factory either in the ghetto or in an urban area subject to the Bradford employment plan. The Economic Development Administration (EDA) or some other agency would provide the insurance company a 90% guarantee of the lease for the life of the lease.

The advantage of the lease guarantee over the loan guarantee is that more of the natural market mechanisms are employed. The *loan* guarantee would involve the user (company operating the factory), the lender (insurance company, and the EDA. The *lease* guarantee adds to this list of interested parties the private builder or developer and is thus very similar to F.H.A. financing of private housing. The private builder represents that specialized group of experts in the field of industrial development whose unique function is to discover, sponsor, develop, and invest, short-term, in industrial development projects. Banks and insurance companies ordinarily do not perform this function. They merely respond to the initiatives of others. Under the current programs those initiatives are taken either by a local non-profit development corporation which is seeking to attract industry to the community but is not expert in the many factors which influence industrial development or by the industrial user who will occupy the plant and therefore has a biased notion of its importance. The balanced judgment of the private developer which comes from his unique expertise and experience is needed.

Under the lease guarantee scheme, the private builder would sponsor and develop a totally equipped plant for lease to an industrial user for periods of up to 30 years. The developer would then apply to EDA through a local development organization for a guarantee of the lease which had been negotiated by the potential user and the builder. If EDA determined that the project would provide long-term employment for the long-term unemployed and that the industrial user could reasonably be expected to be able to make the required rental payments. EDA would unconditionally guarantee the lease for its full term to the extent of 90% of each rental payment. With the consent of EDA the lease would be assignable and thereby enable the builder to obtain long-term financing from an insurance company or other source for the completed plant. In order to make certain that the builder has made an equity investment in the completed project, any financing obtained on the basis of the assignment of the guarantee lease would not exceed 90% of the total initial cost.

In the event of default by the industrial user, the builder would have the option of:

1. Continuing the loan payments while attempting to find a new tenant acceptable to EDA and the long-term lender;

2. Repaying (or refinancing) the debt without EDA's guarantee, or

3. Abandoning the project.

In the latter case, the developer's interest would be conveyed to EDA which would then take possession of the property as it does in defaulted loans under the F.H.A. program.

For its guarantee EDA would receive from the developer an annual premium equal to ¼ of 1% of EDA's future contingent liability (the amount of money EDA could be liable for at any point of time). This premium, plus the earning reserves the premium would bring, together with a 5% reserve of EDA's initial contingent liability, would make it possible for EDA to suffer losses of at least 12%. The 5% reserves figure means a leverage (or a multiplier effect) for EDA's funds of 20 to 1; that is, a $1 million commitment by EDA would be adequate for a $20 million project.

The advantages under the lease guarantee proposal are as follows:

a. The amounts of financial resources that can be allocated to economic development projects are much greater than under existing programs. For instance, under the present S.B.A. program, the leverage is 9-1; under the lease guarantee proposal the leverage is 20 - 1.

b. The additional financial resources for economic development would come from the private sector rather than from increased taxes or appropriations.

c. The expertise and experience of industrial developers would be utilized for the first time providing initiative and imagination which the present programs lack.

d. The management, competence and experience of the long-term investing institutions would be employed to a much greater extent than at the present time, thus providing further needed expertise and experience.

e. The entire program will be far more flexible because the incentives can be easily adjusted to fit current market conditions and social demands.

In short, if the EDA were provided $1 billion annually under this program it could attract $20 billion of private investment into the ghetto each year; over ten years, $200 billion. I am aware that the money market would be directly affected by such a program but the money market is affected daily by Federal monetary decisions. What we need in such matters is a sense of national objectives and priorities.

## B. EXTEND THE GRANT AND LOAN PROGRAMS OF THE ECONOMIC DEVELOPMENT ADMINISTRATION TO THE GHETTO

One of the oldest myths prevailing among city planners is that land costs make industrial development in the city impossible. The Mid-Chicago Economic Development study, previously referred to, looked into this and reported as follows:

> "Land costs do not seem to be the critical factor restricting land development. Insufficient capital improvements, including sewers, roads, and street lights as well as the character of the environment, appear to be more critical factors." (Volume II, page 63.[2])

There is a federal program in existence that does aid cities which qualify as "redevelopment areas" (defined below) in financing capital improvements. This is the Economic Development Administration (EDA) which was created under the Public Works and Economic Development Act of 1965.

The EDA, among other things, does the following:

1. Makes grants of money, not to exceed 80%, to a community for capital improvements directly related to economic development. This includes water and sewer projects, access roads to industrial parks, preparation of industrial parks, harbors, airports, vocational training schools, etc. (It does not include city halls, courthouses, or police stations.) The term "directly related to economic development" means that the EDA does not take into consideration the number of jobs created during the construction job but rather the number of permanent jobs to be created by the investment. In addition to the grant, the EDA can make a loan to the community for the community's share of the project. The loan runs for 40 years at 4-⅝% interest.

2. Makes loans to businesses for 25 years at 4-⅝% interest. The money can be used for land, buildings, machinery and equipment. The EDA provides 65% of the financing, the

local community 5%, the businessman 10% and the remainder of 20% is obtained through normal commercial financing sources. The 20% from commercial financing sources is ordinarily not difficult to obtain once the EDA approves an application because the EDA will subordinate its 65% interest to the commerical sources.

It is important to have an understanding of the term "redevelopment area". This refers to a) a city of over 250,000, or b) a county, or c) a labor market area, each of which has the following economic characteristics:

    a) the unemployment rate is at least 6%, or
    b) there was a median family income in 1966 not in excess of $2254.

Thus, Harlem in New York City, with an estimated unemployment rate close to 20% does not qualify for the EDA programs because a) it is not a city of over 250,000, (although it has a population of near 250,000), b) it is not a county, c) and it is not a labor market area. New York City as a whole lacks the economic conditions required to qualify. These restrictions prevent the extension of the EDA programs to the areas in the country most needing them. Historically these programs have been designed for the economic rehabilitation of the mined-out, timbered-out, rural

113

areas of the country. In other words, it is primarily directed to the communities under 50,000. There are some exceptions. Most notably, the following cities over 100,000 are eligible for EDA assistance (as of March 1, 1967):

| Public Works Grants and Business Loans | Public Works Grants Only |
|---|---|
| San Diego, Calif. | Fresno |
| Newark | Tucson |
| Oakland | San Jose |
| Miami | New Bedford, Mass. |
| Providence | Springfield, Mass. |
| | Paterson, N. J. |

During Fiscal Year 1966 (July 1, 1965 to June 30, 1966) EDA made a total of 754 grants, amounting to almost $292 million. The non-EDA share — largely from communities and banks — amounted to $205 million. Most of this money went for sewer or water system construction, the development of industrial parks, the construction of transportation facilities, or the development of tourism facilities. During the same fiscal year EDA made 62 business loans, totalling $43 million.

*In order to make this program achieve its objective of providing employment for the unemployed, it should be extended to the ghettos where the most serious unemployment situations exist.* A number of bills have been introduced to effectuate this but curiously enough no interest or support have come from civil rights leaders, mayors (other than Mayor Daley of Chicago), or the various associations representing the large cities. It is just another example of how economically unimaginative these various groups still are.

## C. CREATE COMMUNITY DEVELOPMENT CORPORATIONS IN THE GHETTO

A number of people have proposed the creation of Community Development Corporations for the purpose of initiating new housing and business programs in the ghetto. This idea has great merit but it has been apparently presumed that new legislation is required to accomplish this. Actually, the vehicle already exists for the creation of those corporations and for their utilization in a broader way than has been proposed to date.

The vehicle I have in mind is the community development program (called the 502 program because it comes under Section 502 of the Small Business Act) of the Small Business Administration (SBA). Under this program the SBA will lend to a local development corporation, ordinarily but not necessarily non-profit, 80% of the money needed for land, buildings, machinery and equipment for 25

115

years at 5½ interest. The remaining 20% is provided by the local development corporation which obtains its money through stock subscriptions and/or commercial financing. The most usual pattern is for the non-profit corporation to lease the property to a businessman offering him an option to buy at the end of the lease period. The SBA is limited to $350,000 per small business aided. If there were ten small businesses helped by the project, such as an industrial park or shopping center, SBA could provide $3½ million. The important point about this program is that it is applicable to any place in the country without restriction with the exception that it must be used to finance a small business.

The definition of a small business in SBA terms in general is as follows: (1) a retail firm grossing less than $1 million annually; (2) a wholesale firm grossing less than $5 million annually; and (3) a manufacturing firm by rule of thumb, employing fewer than 500 employees. There are different standards for different industries. Thus, in the garment industry 100 employees or less is considered a small business and in the aircraft building industry 1,000 employees or less is considered a small business.

Small business so defined makes up about 96% of all the businesses in the United States.

It employs approximately 40% of the work force and accounts for about one-third of the gross national product. Most people really don't realize that our urban areas are a center of small businesses, not only for retail and wholesaling but for manufacturing as well. 57% of the manufacturing employees in the New York area (1960) worked for concerns with less than 100 employees. The breakdown is as follows:[3/]

| | |
|---|---|
| Firms of 1-3 employees | 16,000 people |
| Firms of 4-7 employees | 34,000 " |
| Firms of 8-19 employees | 108,000 " |
| Firms of 20-49 employees | 222,000 " |
| Firms of 59-99 employees | 187,000 " |
| | 564,000 people |

Looked at another way, in 1964 in the New York area, there were 270,474 businesses of all kinds, including manufacturing. The breakdown, in terms of number of employees, is as follows:[4/]

| No. of Employees | No. of Firms |
|---|---|
| 1 to 3 | 153,649 |
| 4 to 7 | 49,420 |
| 8 to 19 | 38,175 |
| 20 to 49 | 18,009 |
| 50 to 99 | 2,262 |
| 100 to 249 | 3,312 |
| 250 to 499 | 940 |
| 500 or more | 740 |

117

Since the beginning of the program, 65.7% of the 502 loans have gone to manufacturing concerns, 9.7% of the loans went to retail or wholesale businesses, and 18.4% into service industries. 57% of all loans have gone to assist expanding businesses, while 43% went to new businesses. Since the program began (in 1959), 61.1% of all loans have gone into communities that have a population of 5,000 or less, 15.2% into communities between 5,000 and 10,000, 6.2% into communities from 10,000 to 15,000, 5.9% into communities from 15,000 - 25,000, and 11.6% into communities over 25,000 in population.

Here, then, we have an already authorized institution with much experience behind it that can be easily adapted to the ghetto. As noted, very few of these loans have gone into the large city primarily because the larger cities have taken their economic development for granted and have not utilized all the economic tools available. As an example of its application to a large city, the 502 program was skillfully adapted by a group in Chicago headed by Mrs. Muriel Beadle, wife of the president of the University of Chicago, which helped to transform the character of a wide semi-poverty area near the University of Chicago by the construction of one of the most attractive shopping

118

centers in America—the Harper Court Shopping Center.

These community development corporations ordinarily operate without a staff and rely primarily on the experience and expertise of their volunteer Boards of Directors. I would recommend at least a small full-time staff for such a corporation in the ghetto because of the many things it could do. The staff could be funded by the office of Economic Opportunity, the Economic Development Administration, the city, a foundation, or by local contributions. Once again, no legislation is needed; simply imagination and energy.

## D. DIRECT EXISTING PRIVATE AND PUBLIC INVESTMENTS INTO THE GHETTO

There is a great deal that could be done in the city under existing investment programs. For instance, $232,445,000 invested in industrial plants in the New York urban area in 1963[5/] If these investments could be re-directed to the city, much of the needed funds could be provided in the normal course of events. What is needed, of course, is a change of attitude and approach on the part of city planners so that the city's economic opportunities and advantages do not continue to go unnoticed.

119

In Chapter Two, I pointed out a variety of ways in which the city could expand industrial and job opportunities for city and, more particularly, ghetto residents including the following:

1. Utilization of abandoned defense or out of date industrial facilities such as the Brooklyn Navy Yard or Chicago Stockyards.
2. Reclaiming of rivers and harbors by dredging and filling.
3. Rehabilitation of property the city takes title to through seizure for non-payment of taxes.
4. Fuller use of the air rights over public property.
5. Development of multistory and, where feasible, underground factories.
6. Construction of public buildings in ghetto areas.
7. Expansion of badly needed public service employment opportunities to those unsuccessful in the competition for existing jobs.

The only legislation required to accomplish these things is possibly the rezoning of land areas. The rest only requires a little imagination such as that incorporated in the proposed plans for Harlem sponsored by the New York Museum of Modern Art and the others mentioned in Chapter II.

## E. AUTHORIZE INDUSTRIAL BONDS FOR THE GHETTO

Industrial bonds are a form of financing many communities employ for their economic development. With the proceeds of a bond they build a factory and many times equip it. The bonds are tax free because the U. S. Constitution prohibits the federal government from taxing income of a municipality. They have been growing in popularity. From a mere $4 million in 1960, the volume of tax-free industrial financing soared to over $500 million in 1966. In addition, the Securities and Exchange Commission is getting interested because if the companies that were assisted had done the financing publicly instead of the communities, the securities would have had to be registered with the S.E.C.

In 1966, more than half a billion dollars ($500,163,000) were raised by communities to finance municipally owned plants. This was more than double the $211,931,000 of such financing done in 1965. In the first six months of 1967, 69 issues totalling $405,434,000 had been sold. Altogether, 124 bond issues were sold in 1966.[6]

121

Middletown, Ohio, for example, sold $82.5 million of bonds, the largest such issue on record, to finance expansion for the Armco Steel Company. The Camden Industrial Board of Camden, Alabama, sold a $70 million offering to finance papermill facilities for MacMillan, Bloedell & Powell River, Ltd., and the United Fruit Company.

Kentucky, where 24 industrial aid bond issues totalling $107,465,000 were sold, was the most active state in this type of financing. After Kentucky, seven other states sold more than $10 million of industrial aid bonds in 1966: Alabama, $92,413,000; Iowa, $65,000,000; Georgia, $52,000,000; Delaware, $52,000,000; Arkansas, $47,568,000; West Virginia, $24,000,000; Mississippi, $16,165,000; and Kansas, $11,055,000.

Although thirty two states now authorize industrial bonds they are typically utilized only in the smaller communities. Once again, the reason for this is simply that it is the smaller cities and towns that have directed their attention and energies to economic development. The Public Development Corporation of New York City is considering the possibility of financing plants with tax exempt bonds. This is something any community could do without waiting for federal action.

## F. ENACT TAX PRIVILEGES AND INCENTIVES FOR THE ECONOMIC DEVELOPMENT OF THE GHETTO

A city can affect the "supply" of industrial and commercial land through zoning changes; through taxing, the city can affect the "demand" for such land. There are a number of ways in which a city, by adjusting its tax policies, can increase the demand for parcels of land. Just to describe a few:

a. Grant a credit against property taxes for investments in new or modernized plants in ghetto areas.

b. Exempt a manufacturing company in ghetto areas from paying the city's commercial occupancy tax. New York City is considering this.

c. Exempt an industrial company located in the ghetto from paying a city's sales or use tax on purchase of new equipment or reduce the amount of such tax to such companies.

d. Reduce the city income tax to companies employing more than a given number in ghetto areas or exempt such companies from the income tax for a period of years.

e. Reduce assessment on industrial real estate in ghetto areas.

I should hasten to explain that I am well aware that adjusting tax policies to accomplish social goals is a very complicated matter and care must be taken not to rely on tax changes alone.

For instance, the administration of the real estate tax is very difficult. In New York State the state constitution specified assesed values shall not exceed "full value;" the New York City administrative code prescribes assessed values as the selling price under "ordinary circumstances," and the courts mandate that a building cannot be assessed at more than reproduction cost, less depreciations. It is claimed that these inconsistencies may be one of many factors causing assessment variations as much as 100 percent.

Over the years, in response to differing pressures and needs, inequitable tax treatment has developed among broad classes of taxable sources: geographical area, type of land used, taxpayer type, and exemption class. Also, a municipal tax policy must take into consideration a variety of objectives, including: stability of city income, administrative costs, geographical areas, land use patterns, taxpayer types, construction, housing conditions, social and cultural objectives, community aesthetics, city growth, and a just distribution of tax burdens.

What is needed in almost every American city is a complete review of its tax programs and policies in light of changing community values, patterns, needs, and objectives. Perhaps the Model Cities Program will force cities to undergo this review.

The possible tax changes noted above are only a handful of ways in which a city can alter its tax methods for social goals. The tax practices of each city vary so widely that it would be difficult to be both clear and complete in listing all the ways that a city might follow without writing a separate volume. But the few examples cited should suggest to those cities seriously interested in rehabilitating their ghettoes in the near future that tax policies must be addressed when they are considering the land economics of the ghetto because of the direct effect different tax programs have on the demand for such land.

Two final observations on taxation. I caution against complete exemption of all or most taxes of ghetto industrial and commercial land because one of the objectives of an economic development program is not only to employ people and thereby reduce welfare payments but also expand the tax base of the city.

Finally, just as a city may alter its tax policies and programs, so might the state and federal governments. The municipal associations representing our cities and mayors should look very carefully into these possibilities.

## G. INSTITUTE A SET-ASIDE PROCUREMENT PROGRAM FOR THE GHETTO

This is best explained by way of example. The Small Business Administration supervises a "set-aside" program for small business. That is, it works with the federal government procurement agencies such as the Department of Defense, General Services Administration, National Aeronautics and Space Administration, and the Atomic Energy Commission, in setting aside certain procurement contracts for exclusive bidding by small business. Only businesses certified by the Small Business Administration to be small business are qualified to bid on such contracts. Companies that are in the big business category cannot bid. These set-aside contracts amount annually to $2 billion.

What I have in mind is the extension of this concept to the ghetto. That is, require the government procurement agencies to set aside a certain amount of contracts for exclusive bidding by firms, large or small, located in the ghetto.

The procurement agencies would oppose this on the grounds that they would be forced to pay more on these contracts. This is not necessarily true since a requirement could be

126

added, as it is in the small-business set aside contracts, that each procurement must be subject to competitive bidding and must result in a fair price to the government. Of course, the procurement agencies are thinking very narrowly when they argue that government costs would rise under a set-aside program. What they are really saying is that they fear their individual departmental budgets might rise. They do not consider that welfare costs might go down. In terms of overall government costs, a good argument could be made that total government costs would actually go down under a set-aside program.

In any event, there is a Defense Department precedent for special consideration to be given in procurement matters to firms located in "depressed areas;" i.e., areas classified as "redevelopment areas" by the Economic Development Administration. Under Defense Manpower Policy #4, issued July 6, 1960, by the Eisenhower Administration and re-issued Dec. 28, 1962, by the Kennedy Administration, and still in force, "it is the policy of the federal government to encourage the placing of contracts and facilities in areas of persistent or substantial labor surplus." The language, to a person of average intelligence, would appear to be quite clear as to federal policy:

127

"all procurement agencies shall:

(1) Use their best efforts to award negotiated procurement contracts to contractors who will perform a substantial proportion of the production on those contracts within labor surplus areas, giving first preference to contractors performing in persistent labor surplus areas, to the extent that procurement objectives will permit: Provided, That in no case will price differentials be paid for the purpose of carrying out this policy.

(2) Where deemed appropriate, *set aside portions of procurements* for negotiation at prices no higher than those paid on the balance of these procurements exclusively with firms which will perform or cause to be performed a substantial proportion of the production on these contracts within labor surplus areas, giving first preference to firms in persistent labor surplus areas.

(4) In the event of tie-bids or offers on any procurement, award the contract to the firm which will perform a substantial proportion of the contract in persistent or substantial labor surplus areas by incurring costs on account of production or manufacturing in such labor surplus areas (by itself or its first tier subcontractors) that amount to a substantial proportion of the contract price, giving first preference, other things being equal, to the firm that will perform in persistent labor surplus areas.

(5) Encourage prime contractors to award subcontracts to firms which will perform a substantial proportion of the production on those Subcontracts in labor surplus areas, particularly in areas of persistent labor surplus.

As one learns after bitter experience in the Executive Branch of the government policy means nothing without an effective machinery

128

of implementation. The machinery in this instance consists of a low level interagency Committee headed by the Deputy Assistant Director for Manpower of the Office of Emergency Planning (O.E.P.). The Deputy Assistant Administrator for Manpower is at the fourth level below the Director of O.E.P. The function of the Committee is to advise member agencies on how to carry out the policy and to report to the Director of O.E.P. as to progress.

The result, needless to say, is no results. Without any enforcement "teeth" the procurement agencies have paid no attention to the policy. In the winter and spring of 1966-67, a proposal was made to "strengthen" the policy by (1) requiring periodic statistics as to accomplishment with accompanying analysis; (2) Raise the level of the supervisory interagency committee to the level of the Director of O.E.P. (who holds the rank of an Undersecretary); and (3) cause the policy statement to be re-issued by the President rather than by the Director of O.E.P. Even this mild, modest attempt to implement the stated policy of three administrations was too much for the technicians of the Budget Bureau and the Council of Economic Advisers who, up to March, 1967, had succeeded in keeping the issue from the President for decision since September, 1966. Their strategy, of course, was to see that the proposal might, in the classic manner, die for lack of attention and bureaucratic "old age." This cannot be blamed on the President despite his well-known appetite for information on government problems. He cannot possibly keep abreast of everything going on in the Executive Branch. The Bureau of the Budget is the "screening staff" for this purpose and has great ability in keeping from the President or his advisors those problems or recommendations it does not favor. In fact, that is its great source of strength.

As in all these proposals, we are simply offering another possibility to direct and encourage private investment into the ghetto. The trouble with the economists and budget technicians is that since human costs and values are not easily quantifiable they refuse to consider them in preparing a national budget. Fortunately our elected representatives are not so protected by dogma or insulated by position that they cannot fairly accurately serve as the thermometer of a democratic people's feelings and aspirations. All of these proposed changes in program of emphasis will more than likely have to come either from the Congress of municipal governments, both of which are closer to the people than anonymous government technicians.

130

# H. PLAN AND CONSTRUCTION HOUSING PROGRAMS IN THE GHETTO WITH A VIEW TO THEIR ECONOMIC EFFECTS

Housing and construction programs necessarily have ends of their own. But they also have important economic effects and potentialities by virtue of the opportunities they offer for Negro contractors and employees. Just as an employment plan was developed for the E.D.A. in industrial plants for industrial workers, the federal government could require that each construction or rehabilitation project in a ghetto financed in part by federal funds be required to utilize qualified Negro contractors (either as prime - or sub contractors), in a portion of the units being constructed. For instance, a certain percentage of the units could be "set-aside" for Negro contractors living in the affected area in a manner similar to the way federal procurement agencies "set-aside" contracts for bidding exclusively by small businesses. In addition, a minimum percentage of Negro labor living in the affected area should be employed by all the contractors working on the project. This would involve delicate problems with labor unions, but it would undoubtedly develop that they would be receptive to a portion of new construction jobs for their union membership rather than none at all.

I pointed out in Chapter II that new state and local public facility needs in the U. S. between 1966 and 1975 amount to over $100 billion. Housing needs are even greater. In spite of the largest slum clearance and rebuilding program in the United States, the number of unsound housing units in New York City, for example, increased from 599,685 in 1960 to 728,390 in 1965.[7]

We could radically revise the ghetto economy through construction programs if we simply make the most of the economic opportunities they offer.

## I. STRENGTHEN AND EXPAND THE ROLE OF NEGRO OWNED SMALL BUSINESSES IN THE GHETTO

The ghetto economy has five main characteristics:

1. High unemployment
2. Extensive welfare programs
3. Flourishing numbers racket
4. The narcotics trade
5. Very small businesses, half of which are owned by non-resident whites, the Negro-owned half generally poorly managed.

The numbers racket and the narcotics trade have a significance far beyond the amounts of

132

money involved. To an important degree they have attracted some of the natural born entrepreneurship of the ghetto. This is not unusual; many American Irish, Jews, Italians, and other former minority groups would not want to look too far back into their own family genealogies. There is a growing interest in Negro communities in Negro owned and managed small businesses. These offer a natural opportunity for ambitious and risk-taking Negroes to participate in the growing economy of the ghetto. There are real problems to face in this field and they cannot be overlooked.

In 1964, the Drexel Insitute of Technology of Philadelphia initiated a massive study of very small business and small businessmen in Philadelphia.[8] Among other things, the objectives of the study were to review the ecomonic characteristics and behavior of firms with less than four employees and to explore the special problems of businesses owned and operated by members of minority groups.

The Drexel study revealed that while there were about ten Negro-owned businesses - insurance, publishing, catering, cosmetic supplies, and contracting - which were quite successfull, most of the 4,242 Negro businesses of Philadelphia, comprising 9 per cent of the city's total businesses, were marginal in profit-making, stability, and physical condition.

The types of businesses followed the pattern observable in other American cities. Nearly all were retail and service trades, and most were single proprietorships. Personal services were the more numerous; hair-dressing and barbering comprising 24 per cent and 11 per cent, respectively, of the total number of Negroes in business. Luncheonettes and restaurants comprised 11.5 per cent of the total. Many of the businesses would be sub-marginal if free family labor were not available. For example, median annual sales for a sample of Negro-owned beauty shops were $2,500, for Negro-owned lucheonettes, $6,800, and for barber shops, $4,400.

Almost all Negro businesses are located in predominantly Negro neighborhoods, but at least half of the businesses in these neighborhoods are white-owned.

Seventy-seven per cent of Negro businesses are concentrated in three of the city's twenty community business areas. The largest Negro community business area, Area 13, comprises nine square miles in the north-central part of the city. Approximately 200,000 Negroes live there representing 69 per cent of Area 13's total population, and about one-third of the city's total Negro population. Approximately 40 per cent (1,615) of all Negro businesses are located here. The Drexel survey team took

134

a sample of the various types of Negro businesses and rated them by appearance. The meanings of these appearance ratings are as follows:

A. "General appearance of being neat and clean looking; with a large sign and/or window display of some current nature; goods or products properly arranged; appears to have enough stock on hand not necessarily a new store."
B. "General appearance of being neat, but not eye-appealing to the observer; with a sign and/or window display of relatively small size; appearance implies adequacy."
C. "General appearance of being 'rundown', untidy and dirty; paint peeling off walls, plaster coming off ceilings, little or no lighting, no displays to speak of; little stock on hand."

Of all the Negro-owned businesses in Area 13, 12.1 per cent fell in Category A (neat and clean), 35.9 per cent in Category B (not eye-appealing), and 32 per cent in Category C (run-down). Of the six largest categories in that area (groceries and delicatessens, luncheonettes and restaurants, candy and variety stores, barber shops, beauty shops, and other personal services), barber shops had by far the cleanest and neatest appearance. Still, only 17.6 per cent of these were in Category A, 60.6 per cent in Category B, and 21.8 per cent in Category C. The fifteen drug stores classified have the neatest and cleanest appearance of all the businesses surveyed: 60 per cent were in Category A, and 40 per cent in Category B. The results in the other two community business areas with a large number of Negro businesses, Areas 14 and 19, were quite similar to the results in Area 13.

The picture, then, of the Negro in business is that of a small businessman—a very small businessman—generally not a very good businessman and, frankly, to date, not a very significant factor in the Negro community.

The Drexel study makes it quite clear that the central problem concerning the Negro businessman is his management ability, not his financing ability. Financing is a problem, but the management factor precedes it. Nevertheless the following statement by a fairly successful Philadelphia Negro merchant is quite typical of the Negro businessman's attitude toward banks: "Local bankers have not treated Negro businessmen fairly. Most of the time they are willing to lend money only after you have been able to obtain money from some other source. Most of the time they disregard a good credit experience they have had with you prior to the attempt to obtain a significant loan to promote or improve your business."

But prejudice is not the sole reason for the scarcity of capital available for Negro businesses. Bankers, of course, share in and manifest American racist patterns, but they also make many loans to Negroes. In Philadelphia, one large bank has had a branch in a predominantly Negro area for many years. About 50 per cent of the branch customers are Negroes, as are 50 per cent of the time-payment customers. The important point to note is that his bank has been making consumer loans to Negroes for years, and for a long time Negroes have accounted for at least 50 per cent of its consumer lending activity. Contrast this with the fact that this same branch has only two loans to Negro businessmen on its books today. It is obvious that the bank, located in a Negro area and catering heavily to Negro consumer loans, is not discriminating. In fact, all three banks having branches in Negro areas of Philadelphia report they are seldom approached by Negro businessmen for commercial loans.

The financing of home purchases is further evidence that banks and other financial institutions desire to make loans to Negroes. A comprehensive report financed by the Fund for the Republic covering home purchases by Negroes and whites in Philadelphia in 1955 was made by the Institute for Urban Studies, University of Pennsylvania, at the request of the Commission on Race and Housing.[9/] Banks financed approximately 10 per cent of the Negro purchases and 18 per cent of the white purchases. (Savings and Loan Associations accounted for the largest share of the financing for each group.) The report reviewed 1,574 home purchases by Negroes and 443 by whites in that year. These 1,574 purchases accounted for 30 per cent of all purchases by Negroes in Philadelphia that year. The report concluded that "Negroes and whites alike were able to obtain very liberal credit terms, particularly considering the age of the properties on which loans were made. Thus, despite the recency of the transition and the racial mixture of the areas, purchasers appear to have had no unusual difficulties in obtaining the necessary financing for the acquisition of their homes." In fact, the records indicate that Negro purchasers obtained mortgage terms which were somewhat more liberal than those advanced to whites. The reason for this is largely explained by the higher proportion of Veterans Administration and Federal Housing Administration loans made to Negroes.

The reason that Negroes can obtain consumer and mortgage but not commercial financing lies in the different types of financing involved.

A review of the commercial consumer and mortgage lending practices of banks should make this clear.

The economic trend of a locality or the country as a whole is a factor in determining a bank's loan and investment policy. Because of the dynamic nature of business conditions, changes in particular industries or areas can enhance or jeopardize the liquidity and the soundness of a bank. A cautious or conservative policy is generally thought the best insurance against possible swings or fluctuations of the economy.

The banking community recognizes that the making and handling of mortgage and consumer loans differ greatly from the making and servicing of the average commercial loans. Of primary importance in consumer lending is the honesty and ability of the borrower; information in regard to the borrower's assets and indebtedness; the source, amount, adequacy and, above all, the permanency of his income. Mortgage loans, of course, are fully secured by real estate. In making commercial loans to very small businesses, the management ability of the borrower is of highest concern. The financial factor, while important, is generally the most difficult to analyze properly because of the small firm's chronically inadequate or nonexistent records.

In short, the Negro consumer who has a stable income and is not overextended in his credit can get a consumer loan as easily as any non-Negro with the same characteristics. The same is true of a Negro home owner who can provide a first mortgage on his property thus fully securing the loan.

But commercial financing, based on the proven management ability of the borrower in a stable industry and a stable locality, is another thing. It is not only Negroes who have difficulty getting such financing. *Sixty per cent of all businesses in Philadelphia have no borrowing facility from a bank or finance company, irrespective of race.*[10]

The key then to the lack of financing for Negro businesses thus lies in the characteristics of Negro businesses more than in the fact they are Negro-owned.

In February, 1964, the Small Business Administration began an experimental program in Philadelphia called the six-by-six program in which it made loans to businessmen for $6,000 for 6 years with little or no collateral but with a special management program designed for the very small businessman such as is found in the ghetto. A non-profit organization, called the Small Business Opportunities Corporation, was set up to oversee the program and began operation on January 29, 1964. From January 29, 1964 to April 19, 1965, 219 potential and established small businessmen were successful in obtaining loans for a total of $915,572. under the 6 x 6 program. These were selected from the thousands who expressed an interest in the program.

Management assistance was available to all small businessmen regardless of whether or not they wanted an SBA loan. Training was primarily in small business management fundamentals, such as: problems of small business operation, business records, common business tax problems, credit and collections, advertising and sale promotion, and insurance principles. Most of the counseling was by successful businessmen on a one to one basis. Counseling began at the time the loan applicant was interviewed. In many instances, serious counseling was an effective substitute and remedy for the businessman's professed need for financial assistance.

In the first year of operation, 98 loans were made to Negro businessmen (as compared with 7 made over a peroid of 10 years) without a single default. At the same time 110 loans were made to white businessmen with 4 defaults. The program has since been expanded and included in Title IV of the anti-poverty program.

Title IV provides for Equal Opportunity Loans up to $25,000. together with the management training and individual management counseling that should help enterprising Negroes begin in business, to modernize or expand. Small Business Development Centers, similar to the Philadelphia SBOC provide the same counselling. In FY '66 there were 1,689 loans made for a total of $17,625,000. The average size loan was $10,371. As of June 1966, 90 of the loans were delinquent and 43 were in liquidation.

The 6 x 6 program shows how a Government agency can experiment in an untried area so that private institutions which cannot take such an original risk might later utilize the Government experiences for normal commercial purposes. Unfortunately, both the Title IV and the 6 x 6 programs have suffered a retrenchment. The Budget Bureau has never been happy with the existence of any of the SBA programs, much less these; the OEO was never at home with the concept of someone gainfully employing himself as well as others under the Poverty Program, and the SBA has reverted to the notion that small business belongs to small towns contrary to all the evidence, not to speak of historical trends.

In order to strengthen the role of Negro owned small businesses in the ghetto and thereby create not only additional employment opportunities but also symbols of success in contrast to the rest of the ghetto, an aggressive small business program for the ghetto should be developed. It is essential to keep in mind that an important aspect of the ghetto's economic development, as well as the ultimate liberation of the Negro businessman, is the full involvement of normal commercial financial institutions and services in the ghetto. The trade contracts, business opportunities, and financial assistance they can offer are far greater than anything the federal government can devise.

An aggressive small business program for the ghetto should include:

a) Re-institution, re-emphasis, and liberalization of the Title IV and 6 X 6 programs of the SBA.

b) Development of high risk casualty and theft insurance policies by the major insurance companies similar to high risk automobile collision insurance policies. Most casualty and theft insurance companies do not insure in Negro areas; this applies to white businessmen as well as Negroes. A progressive, risk taking businessman cannot operate boldly without such insurance; this is

143

true any place, but especially in the ghetto.

c) The banks must be brought into the commercial financing of the very small business. The SBA has proved that the risk is not as great as feared. Banks have now been offered a further incentive because under Title IV of the Economic Opportunity Act they can obtain 100 percent guarantees by the S.B. A.

d) Franchising arrangements must be encouraged for Negro businessmen. One of the most promising opportunities for young Negroes aspiring for a business career but lacking money and experience is in this field. Franchising is an arrangement by which a firm (the franchiser) which has developed a successful pattern or formula for the conduct of a particular kind of business extends to others (the franchisees) the right to engage in the business provided they follow an established program. Typical examples of franchise arrangements are the Howard Johnson restaurants, A & W Root Beer stands, and Holiday Inn Motels.

Among the services franchisers provide to the franchise operators are the following:

144

(1) location analysis and counsel, (2) store development aid, including lease negotiation, (3) store design and equipment purchasing, (4) initial employee and management training and continuing management counseling, (5) advertising and merchandising counseling and assistance, (6) standardized procedures and operations, (7) centralized purchasing with consequent savings, and (8) financial assistance in the establishment of the business.

Needless to say, the franchisee must provide a financial return of some kind to the franchisor. This may take the form of an initial fee ranging from $1,000 or less to over $100,000. In addition to the fee, or in place of it, the franchisee may pay royalties based upon a percentage of his sales. There are variations from one industry to another. In the case of soft ice cream, for example, the franchisor's principal source of profit is derived from sales of the franchisor's sales of merchandise to his franchisees — such as the mix used in preparing the cream, together with cones, napkins and other accessory items.

In a way, the franchisee is not his own boss because in order to maintain the individuality of his system and to protect its good will, the franchisor usually exercises some degree of continuing control over the operations of his franchisees and requires them to meet stipulated standards of quality. The extent of such control varies. In some cases, franchisees are required to conduct every step of their operation in strict conformity with a manual furnished by the franchisor. In others, there is a very loose arrangement.

Depending on the form of arrangement, control, services offered, etc., the franchise can be an excellent way for a Negro to enter business. The U. S. Commerce Department has developed a Franchise Business opportunities Program. This program identifies franchise firms which do not discriminate on the basis of race, color, religion or national origin in the sales, terms or conditions of their franchises. As of March 6, 1967, 249 franchisors had agreed to the terms of the Commerce Department's program. What is needed now is local encouragement and application of this potentially valuable program by Civil rights leaders, poverty warriors, and municipal officials. It is another good example of how existing tools are lying unused because of a lack of focus and purpose in the area of Negro business and the ghetto economy.

e) Negro businessmen must organize their own business associations until such time as they are freely admitted into the local chambers of commerce and other trade assoications. Such assoications will help give the Negro businessman a sense of identity and a channel of communication for success stories. In addition, they provide a vehicle for representing the individual Negro merchant's views and complaints on rent-gouging, licensing, traffic-routing, and zoning, as well as his interests in the anti-poverty program, city hall, and civil rights.

---

The popularity and success, though short-lived, of the Title IV and 6 X 6 programs offer a valuable new insight into the ghetto which social science researchers with their institutional habituation to welfare programs have failed to disclose—namely, there is talent abounding in large numbers in the ghetto irrespective of the lack of a traditional role model or success symbol in the Negro family. Not every Negro lacks achievement motivation, not every Negro is completely apathetic, not every Negro has given up. The SBA experiments show that the invaluable resources of self-help, initiative and risk-takers are just waiting to be utilized. This to me is the key to the development of the ghetto; namely, the development of local, neighborhood success symbols based on resourceful businessmen and industrious working people. The white establishment not only in the city but more particularly in the Federal Government has got to make a major change in its approach to the ghetto and begin to rely on the ability and self-help determination of the people who live there, shifting from welfare programs to programs based on the Negro's ability to help himself. The SBA experiments show that this can be done. My own experience convinces me that this is what the Negro prefers.

# EPILOGUE

I proclaim it as a matter of the deepest personal faith that somehow the Negro race shall succeed in this country. I proclaim it as an unreconstructed idealist and incurable optimist. I proclaim it as a midwestern egalitarian, a Pope John Catholic, a liberal Democrat, and a Hubert Humphreyite who could still charge up San Juan Hill following one of Hubert's speeches to college people. I proclaim it as a rank amateur student of history and of evolution. Above all, I proclaim it as a frequent witness to the "terrible beauty" of the human spirit that has been made brilliantly visible by black people in the face of oppressive injustice, cruelty, and hatred.

The Negro shall somehow make it in this country. The real question is will the country make it; that is, will the next several generations of Americans elevate the moral quality of American life in line with the requirements for a society with democratic aspirations? In a strange way it can be said that while the racial conflict in the United States is not a happy occasion for the American Negroes it is a healthy phenomenon for the country. It is healthy because it can help purify American democracy much as the McCarthy episode of the 1950's strengthened the nation's commitment to basic civil liberties. The question, therefore, is whether the country can succeed, whether the country as a whole, not the Negro by himself, can further the evolutionary development of a better society of people.

I am proud of America and of America's history. To be sure, there is much to be ashamed of, much to wish were not true, much that has been less than edifying;

but what other country has dared to amalgamate the diversity of ethnic, religious, economic, and geographical groups into a common society as this country has dared to do? While there may be much that is banal and excessively materialistic about the American culture, what other social and economic structure has been as mobile as this country's; or has allowed for the endless opportunity for personal development; or allocated the percentage of its income for the educational, spiritual, and aesthetic betterment of its society? The Negro's demands for justice have been a long time a-coming, at least as far back as the promises made explicit as well as implicit in the Great Charter of 1215. The heaviest burdens of those promises as well as those that followed fell on the United States as it accepted the refugees of European violence and began the first great experiment with the unity of mankind. Or as Eric Hoffer put it more dramatically, "The masses eloped with History to America."

I mention this because in attempting to meet the democratic idea's current challenge we may handicap our efforts by failing to understand ourselves. There is very much in vogue a notion that Americans have always been a violent people and that riots, therefore, are somehow to be expected in times of great social stress. During the summer riots of 1967, the venerable guardian of Western morals, the Manchester Guardian, was moved to observe, "The United States has always been a violent society. In the days of the frontier and of prohibition, in the areas of politics, labor relations, and civil rights, and in liquor and gambling." This from a country whose agricultural policies in the late 1840's and early 1850's caused the deaths of more people through starvation than all of the deaths brought about by all the riots, gold rushes, Indian wars, Western bandits, labor strikes, Chicago gangsters, Mafia, and other social conflicts, including the Civil War, in the entire American history. This is not to speak of the human suffering of forced emigration or the centuries of enslavement by an imperialist colonial policy or even of its own internal disturbances. If the United States has experienced violence, it is only as the westernmost development of a far more terribly violent Western civilization. In short, if our country has received a violent heritage, it has continued it in lesser measure; if it has inherited spiritual and aesthetic impulses, it has generated more: I believe, therefore, that violence is not inevitable.

The real question is still whether this generation of Americans with its Haight-Ashbury's at each end — on the one side, a despairing young set; on the other, a despondent jet set — can collect its constructive energies and construct not an American tragedy but the American dream. There are ample pragmatic arguments: Violence is destructive of past accomplishments, every religion teaches against it, it can never bridge or cement differing cultures, it is hardly the thing for a great society to do, in the era of nuclear power it is centuries out of date.

But essentially the so-called "race question" comes down to the degree of commitment we, as a people, make towards advancing the human idea beyond its present condition; towards stimulating our aspirations and therefore our efforts to excellence, virtue, the good life, our individuality, justice, democracy and peace.

151

For this have mankind's heroes reached for more than they could grasp, its saints hoped for more than they could believe, its poets dreamed for more than they could understand.

The code of human progress was spelled out by an American poet, Oliver Wendell Holmes, in "The Chambered Nautilus":

"Build thee more stately mansions,
  Oh my soul,
As the swift seasons roll,
Leave thy low-vaulted past."

We will have achieving ghettos in this country if we have a truly achieving society.

EUGENE P. FOLEY

152

# SOURCE NOTES

Chapter 1

1. John Brennan, Address to Ancient Order of Hibernians, (Souix City, Iowa, 1886).
2. Max Caulfield, The Eastern Rebellion, (New York, 1963) pp. 133-4.
3. Robert Coles, "The White Northerner." The Atlantic Monthly (June 1966), p. 54.
4. Nathan Glazer and Daniel Patrick Moynihan, Beyond The Melting Pot, (Cambridge, Mass., 1963), p. 36.
5. David Danzig, Racial Esplosion in American Society, New University Thought: Decisions for America (Detroit, 1967)
6. St. Clair Drake, "The Social and Economic Status of the Negro in the U.S., The Negro American, (Cambridge, Mass, 1966), p.16
7. Before Hearings of Senate Committee on Government Operations, Subcommittee on Executive Reorganization, Aug. 30, 1966.
8. Ralph Ellison, Before Hearings of Senate Committee on Government Operations, Subcommittee on Executive Reorganization, Aug. 30, 1966.
9. David Danzig, The Defense of Black Power, Commentary (September 1966)
10. William V. Shannon, The American Irish (New York, 1963).
11. Irving Kristol, The Negro Today is Like the Immigrant Yesterday, N.Y. Times Sunday Magazine (September 25, 1966), p. 128
12. ibid.
13. ibid.
14. Shannon, op. cit.
15. William L. Riordon, Plunkitt of Tammany Hall (New York, 1963), p.6.
16. ibid. p.89.
17. Shannon, op. cit., pp. 143 and 145.
18. ibid. p. 295.

19. Eugene P. Foley, The Negro Businessman, The Negro American, (Cambridge, Mass., 1966), P.563.

20. Samuel Eliot Morison, Oxford History of the American People (New York, 1965), p.666.

21. ibid.

22. W. E. Burghardt DuBois, The Philadelphia Negro, A Social Study (Philadelphia, 1899), pp. 26, 31.

23. Ray Marshall, The Negro and Organized Labor, (New York, 1965)

24. Sadie Tanner Mossell, The Standard of Living Among One Hundred Negro Migrant Families (Philadelphia, 1920), p.9.

25. Herman Miller, N.Y. Times Sunday Magazine, (May 8, 1966), P.30.

26. Kristol, op. cit., p.130.

27. Cleveland Plain Dealer, February 21, 1966.

28. David McClelland, The Achieving Society, (Princeton, N.J.), 1961.

29. ibid.

30. Lauren G. Wispe, Motivational Problems in Training, Occupational Outlook Quarterly, (September, 1965), p.2.

31. Daniel Patrick Moynihan, Employment, Income and the Negro Family, The Negro American (Cambridge, Mass., 1966), p.150.

32. Equality of Educational Opportunity, Office of Education, Department of Health, Education and Welfare (Washington, D.C., 1966), p.22.

33. McClelland, op. cit.

34. Senator Robert Kennedy, Testimony Before the Senate Committee on Government Operations, Subcommittee on Executive Reorganization Hearings, August 15, 1966.

35. Bayard Rustin, Editorial Research Reports (March 8, 1967), p.195.

## SOURCE NOTES

Chapter II

1. Kenneth Clark, Dark Ghetto, (New York, 1965), p.1.
2. Milton Kother, Institute for Policy Studies, Memo #14, (Washington D.C., November, 1966), p. 1.
3. Herbert Hill, Hearings before the New York City Commission on Human Rights, September 24, 1966.
4. Charles E. Silberman, The Myths of Automation, (New York, 1966), p.ix.
5. ibid. p.4.
6. ibid. p.4.
7. ibid. p.1.
8. County and City Data Book, U.S. Bureau of the Census (Washington, D.C., 1967).
9. Metropolis New York, (New York, November, 1966), p.11.
10. ibid. p. 23
11. Dr. Martin McGuire, Unpublished Memorandum, U. S. Commerce Dept.
12. Mid-Chicago Economic Development Study, Vol. I, (Chicago, 1966) pp. 8-9
13. N.Y. Times, January 9, 1967, p. 81.
14. op. cit., County and City Data Book.
15. N.Y. Times, April 19, 1966.
16. op. cit., p. 56.
17. N.Y. Times, September 18, 1966.
18. Violence in the City—an End or a Beginning?, California Governor's Commission on the Los Angeles. Riots, (California, December, 1965).
19. Kenneth Clark, Dark Ghetto, (New York, 1965), p. 41.
20. Hearings before the Senate Committee on Government Operations, Subcommittee on Executive Reorganization, August 29, 1966.
21. George Bernard Shaw, Man and Supermen, (Baltimore, Med., 1952), p. 19.

Chapter III

1. Before the Hearings of the Senate Committee on Government Operations, Subcommittee on Executive Reorganization, December 6, 1966.
2. Mid-Chicago Development Study, Vol. II (Chicago, 1966), p. 63.
3. N.Y.C. Dept. of Commerce and Industrial Development.
4. *ibid.*
5. County and City Data Book, U.S. Bureau of Census (Washington, D.C.).
6. Investment Bankers Association, Research Dept., Washington, D.C.
7. N.Y.C. Dept. of Commerce and Industrial Development.
8. Drexel Institute of Technology, An Analysis of the Little Businessman in Philadelphia, Vol. I, (Philadelphia, 1964), iii.
9. Chester R. Rapkin and William Grissby, The Demand for Housing in Racially Mixed Areas (Berkeley, Calif., 1960), pp. 83-86.
10. *Ibid.* p. 92.